MW01485296

Reading Lessons Through Literature

Level 1

by Kathy Jo DeVore

www.barefootmeandering.com

veritas • gnaritas • libertas

Table of Contents

Section 3: Elson Primer

Appendices   345

Introduction

In the early decades of the 1900s, physician Samuel Orton and psychologist Anna Gillingham identified the main phonograms used to write the English language as part of their method for helping people with reading disabilities. Elementary educator Romalda Spalding, a student of Dr. Orton, later expanded upon the work of Orton and Gillingham to create the Spalding Method of teaching reading, writing, and spelling.

Many other Orton phonogram programs have since been developed which teach reading through spelling. The phonograms—letters or groups of letters which form sounds—represent the forty-five sounds in the English language. Children first learn the phonograms, then they begin spelling. Spelling words are marked according to phonograms and spelling rules. Amazingly, just seventy-five phonograms and thirty spelling rules can be used to explain most English words—98%, in fact. This is an incredible percentage considering that most people believe that English is not a phonetic language.

Why Write Another Orton Phonogram Reading Program?

There are plenty of Orton phonogram programs on the market. My main reason for writing yet another one was that I found the others difficult to implement. I am a mother with five children who range between two years old and seventeen. Whenever it's been time to teach another child to read, I've been either pregnant, had a baby or toddler, or we were moving cross-country.

It shouldn't be surprising that busy mothers often find these programs difficult to implement at first. In the past, some of them have even required the teacher to take a class in order to be able to teach the course. Now, there are more teaching helps available, but they can be expensive.

So the first thing I wanted was something that was pick-up and go. Teaching the phonograms and dictating spelling words is actually very simple and straight forward. The second thing I wanted was a program that focused, quite simply, on the beginning reader, including a list of spelling words that led straight into an inexpensive, easy-to-find set of stories to read. These were the criteria which lead to *Reading Lessons Through Literature*.

Why Teach the Phonograms?

There are those who argue that learning the seventy-five basic phonograms is more than what is necessary to learn to read. Technically, this is true. Children are adaptable, and their flexible little minds often learn things in spite of our teaching mistakes. I'm not arguing that it's the only way to teach reading. I'm arguing that it's the best way to teach reading, for the following reasons:

1. There is a logic to the spelling of the English language, but without learning the basic phonograms and spelling rules, the logic is difficult to see and apply. Learning to read without knowing all of the phonograms is the same as learning to read without knowing the most common sounds of the individual letters, which is to say that while it may be possible, it's far more difficult than it needs to be. With the basic phonograms and thirty spelling rules, the majority of English words can be understood and spelled. Why give children only some of the tools needed for decoding the language? Math would also seem illogical if we were never taught that each number represents a specific quantity.

2. Those who do not teach a complete phonics program which includes all of the basic phonograms often teach some sight words instead. The common list of sight words, called Dolch words because they were compiled by Dr. Dolch in 1948, includes words that can make up 50-70% of a general text. It is commonly, and erroneously, stated that many of these words cannot be sounded out, and therefore must be memorized by sight.

There are 220 Dolch words, 220 words that many children are expected to memorize by sight. Why are 75 basic phonograms considered more difficult than 220 sight words?

3. When programs do not teach all the phonograms, they leave a child with no direction on how to decipher new words which have uncommon phonogram sounds.

4. Proponents of teaching a whole language (sight word heavy) reading program often make a disturbing observation. They point out that children will figure out the phonogram sounds through learning the sight words. In other words, instead of being taught, children are expected to figure it out on their own. No wonder we have a literacy problem in this country.

Necessary Materials

Children learn to both read and write the phonograms in this program. This can be in the optional workbook, on a white board, in a sand tray, or any other method you wish.

Children do need a place to write spelling words. You can either print and use the blank page from the workbook, or purchase a primary composition book for this notebook. Primary composition books are produced by both Mead® and Roaring Spring. If you use the blank page from the workbook, keep the spelling lists separate from the rest of the workbook. Children should read their spelling words daily, so it's best if they don't have to search for them.

Sections

Reading Lessons Through Literature has three sections. Following is an overview of each section.

Section 1. Begin teaching the phonograms. There are some slight differences between Orton programs regarding which phonograms are taught. This program teaches seventy-five basic phonograms.

Section 2. After you've taught the first 26 phonograms (*a* to *z*), begin teaching the spelling words. Simple but explicit instructions are given for having the child start his own spelling notebook. Spelling rules are referred to when applicable. Children can generally learn 10-15 words per week in Kindergarten, 20 words per week in 1st grade, and 40 words per week in 2nd grade.

Section 3. After you've taught the first 200 spelling words (lists 1-A through 1-T), introduce the stories. Spelling lists are arranged around the stories in *The Elson Readers*. The stories are divided into 127 readings which correspond to the spelling lists. A child may read a story when he's learned all the words in a story and he is comfortable reading the words from his spelling notebook. It is fine if he still needs to sound the words out, but he should not be struggling.

Section 1: The Phonograms

Section 1 contains a page for each of the 75 basic phonograms. It is set-up with one phonogram per page in order to make flashcards unnecessary. However, if you prefer flashcards, a set is available in the free Spelling Journal download on my site.

Children begin by learning the basic phonograms. Four to five year olds can learn at least two phonograms per day. Older children can often learn four per day without difficulty.

Each phonogram page has the phonogram with its sound(s) just below it. Next is a sample word for each sound. Finally, on the pages with *qu* and the single letter phonograms, there are very basic instructions for writing the letters of the alphabet in print form using a two line system. It is not important to use my written instructions, but it is important to use specific terminology while teaching the child to write. Precise terminology helps eliminate confusion. It doesn't matter whether you call the bottom line the base line or the ground. What matters is that both you and the child are using the same words.

The examples in this book are in italic handwriting. Italic handwriting is both attractive and simple, using a continuous stroke for lowercase letters instead of lifting the pencil multiple times. It also transitions easily from basic italic to cursive italic, and in my experience, it produces neat handwriting.

But there are also some very good arguments for learning cursive first. Cursive writing prevents reversals and facilitates proper letter spacing. All lowercase letters start in the same place. In addition, cursive first can help the beginning reader by reinforcing the formation of words from left to right, and the hand motions in writing words in cursive form muscle memory patterns which will help with spelling. Explicit instructions are not given for cursive, but I highly recommend the Peterson method (www.peterson-handwriting.com). The *Reading Lessons Through Literature* optional workbook includes both basic italic and Peterson style cursive pages.

The child should learn to read and write two new phonograms each day. The method is simple and follows a multisensory approach. Seeing, hearing, saying, and doing—these are the basics in multisensory learning. Using multiple senses to learn new information helps the brain process the information, which helps children to remember the information better and longer.

- During the oral portion of the lesson, using either the phonogram pages in this book or flashcards, have the child repeat the sound(s) of each phonogram several times while looking at it.

- Before moving to the written portion of the lesson, have the child practice making the phonograms in other ways while saying the sounds. Start with large motions, having him write the phonograms in the air. Move on to smaller motions by having him use his finger to trace the phonograms, either on paper or using sandpaper letters. Use blocks or wooden letters.

- During the written portion of the lesson, have the child say the sound(s) of each phonogram while writing it approximately six to eight times. This can be in the optional workbook, in a composition book, on a white board, in a sand tray, or any other method you wish.

Sample phonogram pages. The left is from the optional workbook. The right is an example of how to set up a phonogram page in a primary composition book.

Learning the phonograms, or even just the basic sounds of the twenty-six letters of the alphabet, is not a simple task. Children *will* forget the sounds, but that's okay. Just keep moving forward and eventually the sounds will stick. Help them with the sounds when they forget. **Do not stop teaching new phonograms, though.** It feels counter-intuitive, but they do not have to know the phonograms perfectly to begin spelling. In fact, using the phonograms in spelling will actually help them remember the phonograms better.

A phonogram can make up to six sounds. Sample words are given to help the instructor identify each sound, but they are only for the instructor, not the child. We do not want to give the child extra steps to wade through, like words or pictures, while trying to remember the sounds. An internet search will yield audio files of the phonograms being spoken. It is important to say only the phonogram sound; remember that *b* says /b/, not /buh/. Also, it is important to teach the sounds of the letters, not the names, as only the sounds are necessary for reading. The names of the letters can be taught later. Once the sounds are firmly memorized, I begin casually referring to the letters by name instead of by their phonogram names. Yes, I have had children who could read before they learned the alphabet song.

The "name" of a phonogram is normally just the sound or sounds that the phonogram makes. However, in some cases, it includes a phrase to help differentiate one phonogram from another with the exact, or almost exact, same sound(s). The phonogram name— the sound(s) plus any identifying phrase—is what the child initially learns to say when he sees that phonogram. For instance, the phonogram *ck* is taught as "/k/, two letter /k/." This differentiates it from *k* which makes the same single sound.

Some phonograms are taught with an applicable spelling rule. For instance, English words do not end in the letter *i*, so the phonogram *ai* is "/ā/, two letter /ā/ that we may not use at the end of English words." After a child has learned this well, he can simply say, "/ā/, two letter /ā/," during reviews. Occasionally, ask, "May it be used at the end of English words?" as part of the review.

Once the first 26 phonograms—*a* through *z*—are learned, children will begin learning spelling words, which then eases them into reading.

Section 2: The Spelling Lists

Begin dictating spelling words after teaching all of the single letter phonograms; the last single letter phonogram is **z**. The spelling lists are made up from some of the most common words in the English language, but they are also arranged around the stories in *The Elson Readers*. This book includes the stories from the Primer.

Children can generally learn 10-15 words per week in Kindergarten, 20 words per week in 1st grade, and 40 words per week in 2nd grade. Full instructions for dictating the spelling lists are in Section 2. The following is just a basic overview.

Begin dictating 10-15 spelling words per week to the child while continuing to teach two new phonograms per day. You can dictate two or three words per day, five words two or three times per week, or any combination that works for you. For children still developing fine motor control, a few words every day can help them exercise those muscles without the stress that more writing would cause.

The child will be creating his own spelling notebook. He should read his spelling words daily. The spelling lists give explicit instructions for both student and instructor, but it is assumed that the instructor will also learn the phonograms.

1-A	
top	not
but	hat
cat	bed
red	ran
six	run

Read each word out loud. Pronounce each word carefully, exaggerating any vowel sounds that tend to be garbled in normal speech. Give the word to the child phonogram by phonogram until he has written the word, and then have him read the word aloud. Phonograms are marked according to which of their sounds they make in a given word and by which spelling rules apply to them.

Section 3: The Readers

After you've taught the first 200 spelling words (lists 1-A through 1-T), introduce the stories. Spelling lists are arranged around the stories in *The Elson Readers*, each list corresponding to the story of the same number. Section 3 in this book contains the twenty-nine stories from the Primer. Because the spelling lists are organized around the stories, a child will not encounter a word in his reading until he has first analyzed the word or base word as a spelling word. A child may read a story when he's learned all the words in a story and he is comfortable reading the words from his spelling notebook. It's okay if he still needs to sound out the words, but he should not be struggling.

The Elson Readers include traditional stories, folk tales, and fables; stories about nature and festivals; and poetry including Mother Goose rhymes and poems by poets such as Christina G. Rossetti and Robert Louis Stevenson. Retellings of old tales have been simplified, but not dumbed down.

I have made some changes to these classic readers. Archaic animal names have been changed to reflect the more common modern names. I've made other minor changes in punctuation and wording; however, the stories remain the same. And finally, I've removed the majority of the pictures, usually leaving only one per story. While the original artwork by L. Kate Deal is quite charming, I believe that it's best that beginning readers do not have picture clues to the text. That can encourage guessing instead of practicing decoding skills.

In the Primer, the multi-letter phonograms are underlined. The stories also have multi-syllable words written with the syllables separated for two reasons. First, this supports the beginning reader in reading longer words while he's still learning. Second, because some rules explain when vowels say their long sounds in syllables, seeing the syllables reinforces those rules.

Monday	Tuesday	Wednesday	Thursday	Friday
Review Phonograms	Review Phonograms	Phonogram Quiz	Review Phonograms	Phonogram Quiz
Learn 2 New Phonograms	Learn 2 New Phonograms	Learn 2 New Phonograms	Learn 2 New Phonograms	Learn 2 New Phonograms

Daily Tasks

See very general sample schedules at left and in Section 2. More specific sample schedules are in Appendix D.

While working through Section 1:

1. Review orally all the phonograms which have been learned.

2. Learn to read and write two new phonograms. During the oral portion of the lesson, have the child say the sound(s) of each phonogram while looking at it. Air write and finger trace the phonograms. During the written portion of the lesson, have the child say the sound(s) of each phonogram while writing it. This can be in the workbook, on a white board, in a sand tray, or any other method you wish.

After you've taught all of the phonograms, review the letters of the alphabet while teaching capital letters in the same way.

3. Twice a week, have a phonogram quiz. Call out the phonograms while the child writes them. Again, use any method of writing that you wish. If necessary, give a hint on how to start the first letter of the phonogram, or you may show the phonogram briefly.

When you begin spelling, after learning the phonogram z:

4. Every day, read all of the spelling words already learned.

5. Dictate 10-15 new spelling words per week to the child, phonogram by phonogram. Explicit instructions are given in the spelling section.

17

When you begin reading the stories:

6. Read, and re-read, the stories. I recommend that new readers read each story at least twice. Once the child is reading more fluently, it is enough to read each story only once. If you have a child who finds reading the same story twice more frustrating than encountering new words, by all means, skip the second reading. He may, however, find a second reading more enjoyable than just reading his spelling notebook.

Although the spelling lists are arranged around the stories in *The Elson Readers*, they are also padded with words from the Ayres List, a list of a thousand of the most commonly used words in the English language. Each list in this level corresponds to stories from the Primer and includes ten new words. Not all of these words will appear in the stories.

Slowing the Pace or Taking a Break

If you take a break from new lessons, it is recommended that you continue to review the phonograms and spelling words already learned. This can be done orally in a small amount of time.

Stay the Course

A new homeschooling mother asked, "Which reading program will teach my child to read?" An experienced homeschooling mother replied, "The third one."

Sometimes, we change curricula because we read new research or we learn new information. But other times, we simply don't give a program time to work. Learning to read takes time, and it also relies on the developmental readiness of the child. If the methodology behind a program is sound, then there is no reason to switch programs. Reading is hard work and requires lots of practice. Whatever program you use, give it time to work.

Phonograms
& Spelling Rules

75 Basic Phonograms

a	/ă/, /ā/, /ä/	at, acorn, wasp
b	/b/	but
c	/k/, /s/	cat, city
d	/d/	dog
e	/ĕ/, /ē/	best, me
f	/f/	four
g	/g/, /j/	garden, gem
h	/h/	hat
i	/ĭ/, /ī/, /ē/, /y/	igloo, ice, radio, onion
j	/j/	jam
k	/k/	kite
l	/l/	lot
m	/m/	mat
n	/n/	no
o	/ŏ/, /ō/, /oo/	pot, go, to
p	/p/	put
qu	/kw/	queen
r	/r/	run
s	/s/, /z/	sass, has
t	/t/	tap
u	/ŭ/, /ū/, /ü/	umbrella, unit, put
v	/v/	vowel
w	/w/	water
x	/ks/	fox
y	/y/, /ĭ/, /ī/, /ē/	yellow, gym, sky, baby
z	/z/	zoo
ai	/ā/ — 2 letter /ā/ we may NOT use at the end of English words	hail
ar	/är/	car
au	/ä/ — 2 letter /ä/ that we may NOT use at the end of English words	pauper
augh	/ä/, /af/	caught, laugh
aw	/ä/ — 2 letter /ä/ that we MAY use at the end of English words	paw
ay	/ā/ — 2 letter /ā/ that we MAY use at the end of English words	play
bu	/b/ — 2 letter /b/	build
ch	/ch/, /k/, /sh/	church, Christ, chef
cei	/sē/	receive

ci	/sh/ — short /sh/ ("short" because it begins with a short letter)	facial
ck	/k/ — 2 letter /k/	back
dge	/j/ — 3 letter /j/	dodge
ea	/ē/, /ĕ/, /ā/	beat, dread, break
ear	/er/ as in pearl	pearl
ed	/ed/, /d/, /t/	waded, slammed, picked
ee	/ē/ — double /ē/	tee
ei	/ā/, /ē/, /ī/	their, protein, feisty
eigh	/ā/, /ī/	eight, height
er	/er/ as in her	her
ew	/oo/, /ū/	dew, few
ey	/ā/, /ē/	they, key
gn	/n/ — 2 letter /n/ that we use at the beginning or the end of a word	gnarl, sign
gu	/g/, /gw/	guest, language
ie	/ē/	thief
igh	/ī/ — 3 letter /ī/	sight
ir	/er/ as in dirt	dirt
kn	/n/ — 2 letter /n/ that we use only at the beginning of a base word	know
mb	/m/ — 2 letter /m/	comb
ng	/ng/	ding (nasal sound)
oa	/ō/ — 2 letter /ō/	boat
oe	/ō/, /oo/	doe, shoe
oi	/oi/ that we may NOT use at the end of English words	toil
oo	/oo/, /ŭ/, /ō/	food, hook, floor
or	/or/	cord
ou	/ow/, /ō/, /oo/, /ŭ/, /ü/	our, four, tour, famous, could
ough	/ŏ/, /ō/, /oo/, /ow/, /uff/, /off/	bought, dough, through, bough, rough, cough
ow	/ow/, /ō/	plow, bow
oy	/oi/ that we MAY use at the end of English words	toy
ph	/f/ — 2 letter /f/	phonics
sh	/sh/	shell
si	/sh/, /zh/	transgression, vision
tch	/ch/	clutch
th	/th/, /TH/	think, that
ti	/sh/ — tall /sh/ ("tall" because it begins with a tall letter)	nation
ui	/oo/	fruit
ur	/er/ as in turn	turn
wh	/wh/	wheel
wor	/wer/	worm
wr	/r/ — 2 letter /r/	wreck

30 Spelling Rules

Vowel and Vowel Sound Rules

1. *Q* always needs *u*, and *u* is not a vowel here.
2. *C* says /s/ before *e*, *i*, and *y*. Otherwise, *c* says /k/: picnic, picnicking.
3. *G* may say /j/ before *e*, *i*, and *y*. Otherwise, *g* says /g/.
4. Vowels *a*, *e*, *o*, *u* usually say /ā, ē, ō, ū/ at the end of a syllable.
5. Vowels *y* and *i* may say /ĭ/, /ī/, or /ē/ at the end of a syllable.
6. Vowel *y* says /ī/ at the end of a one-syllable word: by, sky, why.
7. Vowel *y* says /ē/ only at the end of a multi-syllable word: baby, candy.
8. Vowels *i* and *o* may say /ī/ and /ō/ when followed by two consonants.
9. At the end of a base word, /ā/ is usually spelled *ay*. There are ten exceptions when /ā/ is spelled *ey*: convey, hey, ley, obey, osprey, prey, purvey, survey, they, whey.
10. At the end of words, vowel *a* says its third sound: ma, zebra.
11. The *gh* phonograms *augh*, *ough*, *igh*, and *eigh* can each be used only at the end of a base word or before the letter *t*. The *gh* is either silent or it says /f/.

End of Base Word Rules

12. Engish words do not end in *i*, *u*, *v*, or *j*, but YOU and I are special.
13. Phonograms *dge* and *ck* are used only after a single vowel which says its short sound.
14. Phonogram *tch* is used only after a single vowel which does not say its long sound.
    Phonogram *tch* is the phonogram usually used to say /ch/ following a single vowel at the end of base words, but *ch* says /ch/ after a single vowel at the end of six base words: attach, spinach, rich, which, much, such. Phonogram *ch* is used at the end of base words following two vowels (teach, preach) and after a vowel followed by a consonant (church, bunch).
15. We often double *f*, *l*, and *s* after a single vowel at the end of a base word. We sometimes double other letters.

5 Reasons for Final Silent E

16. (1) The vowel says its name because of the *e*.
17. (2) English words do not end in *v* or *u*.
18. (3) The *e* makes *c* say /s/ or *g* say /j/.
19. (4) Every syllable must have a written vowel.
20. (5) Miscellaneous silent *e* covers all other silent *e* usages. This can include preventing a word that would otherwise end in *s* from looking plural, making a word appear larger, making *th* say /TH/, and making homonyms appear different.

Affix Rules

21. When added to another syllable, the prefix all- and the suffix -full each drop an *l*: almost, truthful.
22. When adding a vowel suffix, drop the final silent *e* unless it is still necessary according to other spelling rules, such as making *c* say /s/ or *g* say /j/: charge, chargeable, charging.
23. When adding a vowel suffix to a word ending in one vowel followed by one consonant, double the last letter only if the word is one syllable or the last syllable is accented: begin, beginning; worship, worshiping. Do not double *x*, *w*, or *y*.
24. The single vowel *y* (not part of a multi-letter phonogram) changes to *i* before adding any ending unless the ending begins with *i*: happy, happiness; try, tries, trying. This is because...
25. English words cannot have two letters *i* in a row.
26. To form the past tense of regular verbs, add *ed*. *Ed* forms a new syllable when the base word ends in *d* or *t*. Otherwise, *ed* says /d/ or /t/.
27. Use *s* to make regular nouns plural and to make the third person singular form of a regular verb. Use *es* after phonograms that hiss: *s*, *ch*, *sh*, *x*, and *z*. Refer to rule 23 when adding *es*. *Ch* does not hiss when it says /k/: stomach, stomachs.

Spelling Sh Rules

28. *Sh* spells /sh/ at the begininning of words and at the end of syllables. It never spells /sh/ at the beginning of any syllable after the first one except for the ending —ship: she, fish, hardship.
29. *Ti*, *si*, and *ci* say /sh/ at the beginning of any syllable except the first one. Look to the root word to determine which one to use: par*t*, par*ti*al; transgres*s*, transgres*si*on; fa*c*e, fa*ci*al.

Miscellaneous Rule

30. *Z* says /z/ at the beginning of a base word, never *s*.

C

/k/, /s/

/k/ — cat
/s/ — city

Start at the dotted line and make a small curve down to the ground.

a

/ă/, /ā/, /ä/

/ă/   —   at
/ā/   —   acorn
/ä/   —   wasp

Start at the dotted line, make a small curve down to the ground, go back to the beginning, then go straight down to the ground.

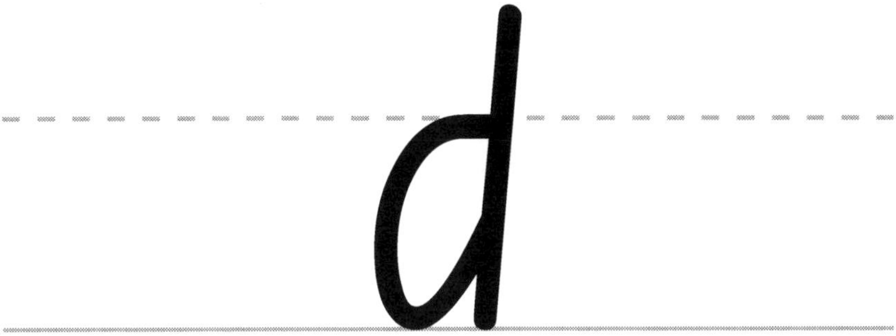

d

/d/

/d/ — dog

Start at the dotted line, make a small curve down to the ground, go back to the beginning, then go straight up into the air and back down to the ground.

g

/g/, /j/

/g/ — garden
/j/ — gem

Start at the dotted line, make a small curve down to the ground, go
back to the beginning, then go down underground and make a hook.

O

/ŏ/, /ō/, /oo/

/ŏ/	—	pot
/ō/	—	go
/oo/	—	to

Start at the dotted line, make a small curve down to the ground and then curve back around to the beginning.

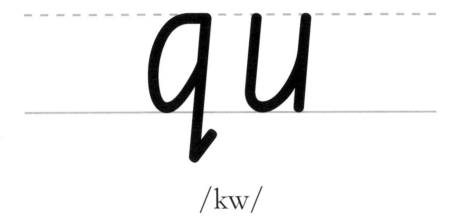

/kw/

/kw/ — queen

This is our first two letter phonogram. Start at the dotted line, make a small curve down to the ground, go back to the beginning, then go down underground and kick. For the second letter, start at the dotted line, go down to the ground, turn around and go back to the dotted line, then go straight down to the ground again.

i

$$/\breve{\imath}/, /\bar{\imath}/, /\bar{e}/, /y/$$

/ĭ/	—	igloo
/ī/	—	ice
/ē/	—	radio
/y/	—	onion

These sounds are the same as those of **y**, only the order is different. To improve memory retention, chant:

/ĭ/, /ī/, /ē/   [pause]   /y/

Start at the dotted line and go straight down to the ground. Then put a little dot on top.

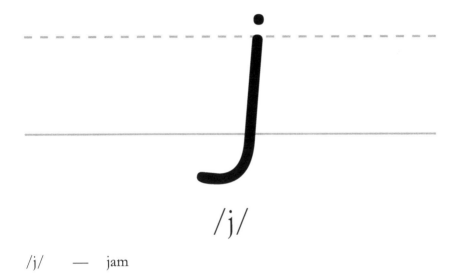

/j/

/j/ — jam

Start at the dotted line, go straight down underground, and make a hook. Then put a little dot on top.

/m/

/m/ — mat

Start at the dotted line, go straight down to the ground, then come back up again to make two humps. /m/ is the two-hump camel.

/n/

/n/ — no

Start at the dotted line, go straight down to the ground, then come back up again to make one hump. /n/ is the one-hump camel.

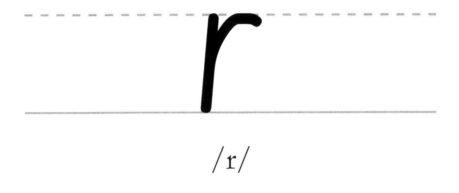

/r/

/r/ — run

Start at the dotted line, go straight down to the ground, then come back up again to make a small shelf.

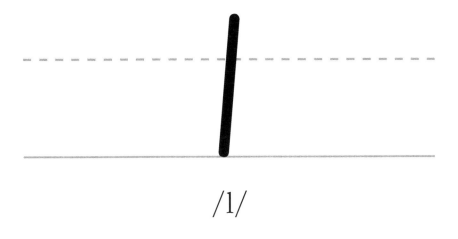

/l/

/l/   —   lot

Start up in the sky and then go straight down to the ground.

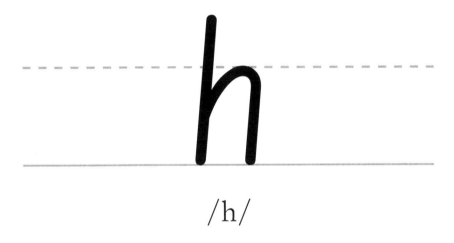

/h/

/h/ — hat

Start up in the air, go straight down to the ground, then come back up again to make a hump.

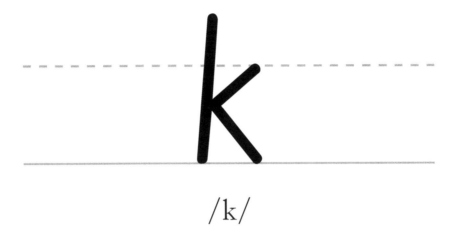

/k/

/k/ — kite

Start up in the air and then go straight down to the ground. Then, pick up the pencil, start at the dotted line and slide down to the line you made, then slide down to the ground.

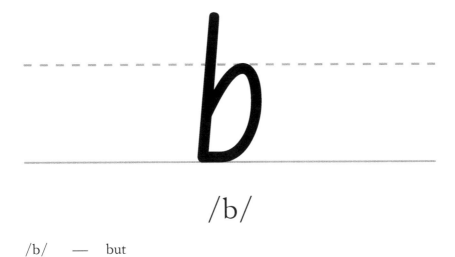

/b/

/b/ — but

Start up in the air, go straight down to the ground, then come back up to the dotted line and make a small curve.

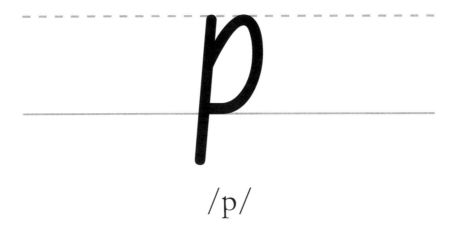

/p/

/p/ — put

Start at the dotted line, go straight down underground, then come back up to the dotted line and make a small curve.

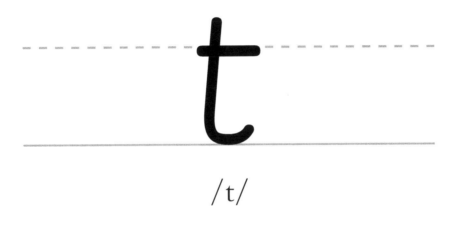

/t/

/t/ — tap

Start up in the air, go straight down to the ground, then walk away. Then pick up the pencil and cross it.

u

/ŭ/, /ū/, /ü/

/ŭ/   —   umbrella
/ū/   —   unit
/ü/   —   put

Start at the dotted line, go down to the ground, turn around and go back to the dotted line, then go straight down to the ground again.

/y/, /ĭ/, /ī/, /ē/

/y/	—	yellow
/ĭ/	—	gym
/ī/	—	sky
/ē/	—	baby

These sounds are the same as those of *i*, only the order is different. To improve memory retention, chant:

/y/   [pause]   /ĭ/, /ī/, /ē/

Start at the dotted line, go down to the ground, turn around and go back to the dotted line, then go straight down underground and make a hook.

e

/ĕ/, /ē/

/ĕ/ — best
/ē/ — me

Start in the middle between the dotted line and the ground, then travel to the dotted line and make a small curve back to the ground.

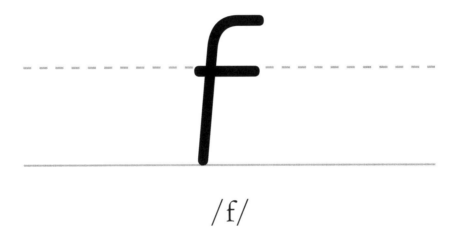

/f/

/f/ — four

Start up in the air and curve down to the ground. Then pick up the pencil and cross it.

S

/s/, /z/

/s/ — sass
/z/ — has

Start traveling at the dotted line, turn around, then turn around again.

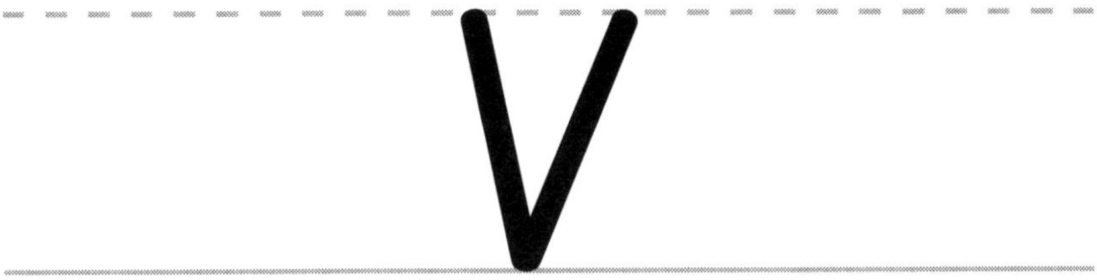

V

/v/

/v/ — vowel

Start at the dotted line, slide down to the ground, then slide up to the dotted line.

W

/w/

/w/ — water

Start at the dotted line, slide down to the ground, slide up to the dotted line, slide down to the ground, then slide up to the dotted line again.

/ks/

/ks/ — fox

Start at the dotted line and slide down to the ground. Then pick up the pencil, start at the dotted line, and slide down to the ground in the opposite direction.

Z

/z/

/z/ — zoo

Walk across the dotted line, slide down to the ground, then walk across the ground.

Begin Section 2.

th

/th/, /TH/

/th/ — think (motor off)

/TH/ — that (motor on)

ck

/k/ — 2 letter /k/

/k/ — back

ai

/ā/ — 2 letter /ā/ that we may NOT
use at the end of English words

/ā/   —   hail

ay

/ā/ — 2 letter /ā/ that we MAY use at the end of English words

/ā/   —   play

sh

/sh/

/sh/ — shell

ng

/ng/

/ng/ — ding (nasal sound)

ee

/ē/ — double /ē/

/ē/ — tee

OO

/oo/, /ü/, /ō/

/oo/	—	food
/ü/	—	hook
/ō/	—	floor

o u

/ow/, /ō/, /oo/, /ŭ/, /ü/

/ow/ — our
/ō/   — four
/oo/ — tour
/ŭ/   — famous

/ü/   — could, should, would

[Note: Although the /ü/ sound occurs only in the above three base words, it is included in order to avoid making these common base words exceptions.]

O W

/ow/, /ō/

/ow/ — plow
/ō/ — bow

ar

/är/

/är/ — car

ch

/ch/, /k/, /sh/

/ch/ — church
/k/ — Christ
/sh/ — chef

au

/ä/ — 2 letter /ä/ that we may NOT use at the end of English words

/ä/ — pauper

aw

/ä/ — 2 letter /ä/ that we MAY use at the end of English words

/ä/ — paw

oi

/oi/ that we may NOT use at
the end of English words

/oi/   —   toil

oy

/oi/ that we MAY use at the
end of English words

/oi/ — toy

er

/er/ as in h<u>er</u>

/er/   —   her

The four spellings of /er/: Oyst<u>er</u>s t<u>ur</u>n d<u>ir</u>t into p<u>ear</u>ls.

ur

/er/ as in t<u>ur</u>n

/ur/ — turn

The four spellings of /er/: Oyst<u>er</u>s t<u>ur</u>n d<u>ir</u>t into p<u>ear</u>ls.

ir

/er/ as in d<u>ir</u>t

/er/   —   dirt

The four spellings of /er/: Oyst<u>er</u>s t<u>ur</u>n d<u>ir</u>t into p<u>ear</u>ls.

ear

/er/ of pearl

/er/ — pearl

The four spellings of /er/: Oyst<u>er</u>s t<u>ur</u>n d<u>ir</u>t into p<u>ear</u>ls.

wor

/wer/

/wer/ — worm

wh

/wh/

/wh/ — wheel

ea

/ē/, /ĕ/, /ā/

/ē/   —   beat
/ĕ/   —   bread
/ā/   —   break

or

/or/

/or/ — cord

ed

/ed/, /d/, /t/

/ed/ — waded
/d/ — washed
/t/ — picked

[Note: **Ed** is the ending used to form the past tense of regular verbs. **Ed** forms a new syllable when the base word ends in **d** or **t**. Otherwise, **ed** says /d/ or /t/.]

ew

/oo/, /ū/

/oo/ — dew
/ū/ — few

cei

/sē/

/sē/ — receive

gu

/g/, /gw/

/g/ — guest
/gw/ — language

wr

/r/ — 2 letter /r/

/r/ — wreck

augh

/ä/, /ăf/

/ä/ — caught
/ăf/ — laugh

ui

/oo/

/oo/ — fruit

oa

/ō/ — 2 letter /ō/

/ō/ — boat

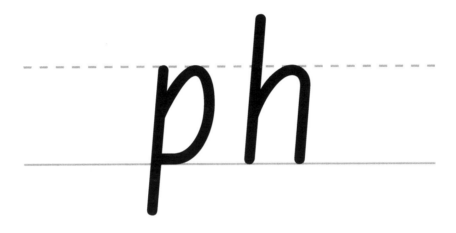

/f/ — 2 letter /f/

/f/ — phonics

oe

/ō/, /oo/

/ō/   —   doe
/oo/   —   shoe

tch

/ch/

/ch/ — clutch

dge

/j/ — 3 letter /j/

/j/   —   dodge

ey

/ā/, /ē/

/ā/ — they
/ē/ — key

bu

/b/ — 2 letter /b/

/bu/ — build

ei

/ā/, /ē/, /ī/

/ā/	—	their
/ē/	—	protein
/ī/	—	feisty

eigh

/ā/, /ī/

/ā/	—	eight
/ī/	—	height

ci

/sh/ — short /sh/

"short" because it begins with a short letter

/sh/ — facial

ti

/ sh/ — tall /sh/

"tall" because it begins with a tall letter

/sh/ — nation

si

/sh/, /zh/

/sh/ — transgression
/zh/ — vision

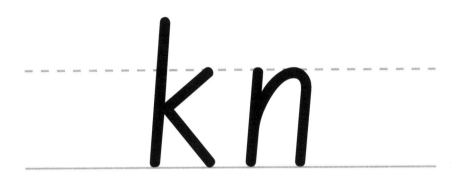

/n/ — 2 letter /n/ that we use only at the beginning of a base word

/n/   —   know

igh

/ī/ — 3 letter /ī/

/ī/   —   sight

ie

/ē/

/ē/ — thief

gn

/n/ — 2 letter /n/ that we can use at
the beginning or the end of a word

/gn/ — gnarl, sign

ough

/ŏ/, /ō/, /oo/,
/ow/, /ŭff/, /ŏff/

/ŏ/	—	bought
/ō/	—	dough
/oo/	—	through
/ow/	—	bough
/ŭff/	—	rough
/ŏff/	—	cough

m b

/m/ — 2 letter /m/

/m/ — comb

Spelling
Lists

The Spelling Lists

The spelling lists are made up of some of the most common words in the English language, and they are arranged around the stories in *The Elson Readers*.

The child will be creating his own spelling notebook. You can either print and use the blank page from the optional workbook or purchase a primary composition book. Primary composition books are produced by both Mead® and Roaring Spring. The following pages give an overview of making the spelling notebook, and the spelling lists give explicit instructions for both student and instructor. Each word is read aloud, then given to the child phonogram by phonogram until he has completed the word. He then reads the word aloud. Phonograms are marked according to which of their sounds they make in a given word and by which spelling rules apply to them.

With five year old, Kindergarten age children, dictate 10-15 new words each week while continuing to teach two new phonograms per day. This can be five words two or three times per week, but if the child has trouble writing five words per day, dictate two to three new words every day.

With six to seven year old, first grade age children, dictate 20 new words to the child each week. This can be five words, four days per week, or it could be ten words twice a week.

Seven to eight year old, second grade children, can handle 40 to 50 words per week, ten words four or five days a week.

If you take a break, continue reviewing the phonograms and spelling words already covered.

In addition to the phonograms, there are also 30 spelling rules. The spelling rules are mentioned when applicable to a spelling word.

The next two pages give sample schedules and sample spelling notebook pages.

Monday	Tuesday	Wednesday	Thursday	Friday
Review Phonograms	Review Phonograms	Phonogram Quiz	Review Phonograms	Phonogram Quiz
Learn 2 New Phonograms	Learn 2 New Phonograms	Learn 2 New Phonograms	Learn 2 New Phonograms	Learn 2 New Phonograms
Read Spelling Words	Read Spelling Words	Read Spelling Words	Read Spelling Words	Read Spelling Words
Dictate 2-3 New Spelling Words	Dictate 2-3 New Spelling Words	Dictate 2-3 New Spelling Words	Dictate 2-3 New Spelling Words	Dictate 2-3 New Spelling Words

Monday	Tuesday	Wednesday	Thursday	Friday
Review Phonograms	Review Phonograms	Phonogram Quiz	Review Phonograms	Phonogram Quiz
Learn 2 New Phonograms	Learn 2 New Phonograms	Learn 2 New Phonograms	Learn 2 New Phonograms	Learn 2 New Phonograms
Read Spelling Words	Read Spelling Words	Read Spelling Words	Read Spelling Words	Read Spelling Words
Dictate 5 New Spelling Words		Dictate 5 New Spelling Words		(Optional) Dictate 5 New Spelling Words

I-A   **I-B**

I-A	I-B
top	and
but	all [3]
cat	tall [3]
red	am
six	be
not	a
hat	an
bed	the [2]
ran	is [2]
run	has [2]

I-A

top
but
cat
red
six

not
hat
bed
ran
run

Analyzing the Spelling Words

We use markings to analyze the spelling words. All of these markings are shown and explained next to the spelling words in the lists. You do not have to know and understand all of the markings in advance. Following are some of the most common markings used. The first two have a note included in the first twenty reading lists; after that, the word is simply marked. The others always have a note included. Notes in brackets [ ] are for the instructor, not the child.

1. When a phonogram does not say its first sound, put a small number above it to show which sound it makes.

3
all

2. Underline multi-letter phonograms.

fi<u>sh</u>

3. Double underline silent letters. The most common is the final silent *e* at the end of words. Final silent *e* has different functions, and these functions are often marked and discussed with the word. For instance, Reason 1 silent *e* makes the vowel say its name, so a bridge is drawn from the silent *e* to the vowel.

min<u>e</u>

The other reasons for silent *e* are marked with a number beside the double underline and discussed with the word. You can see the rules on page 23 for a list of all the reasons for a final silent *e*. Reason 5 is a miscellaneous silent *e*, but the others have specific reasons.

<u>are</u>₌₅   Double underline the silent *e*.

4. Underline *a, e, i, o*, and *u* when they say /ā/, /ē/, /ī/, /ō/, and /ū/ at the end of a syllable.

m<u>e</u>

5. Mark eXceptions, phonograms which don't say any of their normal sounds, with an X.

X
of

180

Dictating the Spelling Words

1. Say the word, then say the word in a sentence if necessary or desired. I only make up a sentence when my child doesn't understand the word or when the word is a homonym.

2. Call the word out phonogram by phonogram. Give the child time to write each phonogram. Correct as necessary. If the child can't remember a phonogram, give a reminder. A white board is handy for this, but you could also use a flashcard, the phonogram pages at the front of this book, or just a sheet of paper.

For example:

top	Top. The first phonogram is /t/. The next phonogram is /ŏ/, /ō/, /oo/. The last phonogram is /p/. /t/-/ŏ/-/p/. Top.
3 all	The first phonogram is /ă/, /ā/, /ä/. Write a small 3 above it to show that it says its third sound. The next phonogram is /l/. The last phonogram is /l/. We often double /l/ after a single vowel at the end of a base word. /ä/-/l/-/l/. All.
b̲e̲	The first phonogram is /b/. The next phonogram is /ĕ/, /ē/. Underline /ē/; *e* says /ē/ at the end of a syllable.

3. Have the child read the word.

Follow this format every time. After the first few words, only the additional information, such as the markings and references to spelling rules, are included.

It's important to note that this program is built upon repetition and practice. Applicable spelling rules are given with the spelling words. Over time, instructor and student will both learn these rules just from hearing and saying them so often during spelling dictation.

As you both become more comfortable with the procedure, it is also a good practice to ask the child questions to get him analyzing the words. For example:

Instructor: Is *a* making its first, second, or third sound?

Student: Second.

Instructor: It's making its second sound, so write a small 2 above it.

———————

Instructor: Why do we need the silent *e*?

Student: Silent *e* makes *i* say /ī/.

Instructor: Double underline the silent *e*, then draw a bridge between the silent *e* and *i*.

Reading the Spelling Words

Children should read their spelling words frequently. That means daily at first. Once children have 200 words—lists 1-A through 1-T— they can begin reading the stories. At that point, you might alternate. Twice a week, a child can read the new story, and on the other days, he can read his spelling words.

Once the list reaches 250 to 300 words, the list can be split into parts. For instance, have the child read the most recent 100 words, and then review 100 older words. The important part is to have the child continue practicing by reading daily.

Sounding Out and Lazy vowels

Some words are exceptions. This means that one of its phonograms does not make any of its normal sounds. We (sometimes) mark these phonograms with an X, but that does not help the child remember the sound. I have had my children sound them out as if the word was normal. This gives them an audio clue.

As an example, let's look at the word **one**. When the child learns **one** on the spelling list, we tell him, "Think to spell /ōn/." Later, when he comes across it on his spelling list, we might say, "This phonogram is an exception, but sound it out as if silent *e* were making *o* say /ō/, /ō-n/. That's how the word used to be pronounced, but now we say /wŏn/." We can also teach that these exception words have two names, their real names and a nickname. We sound out the real name, but we call them by their nicknames.

In 127 spelling lists, there are 1,720 words, and less than ten exceptions. I actively avoid marking exceptions because it seems that children have an easier time remembering the "nickname" after sounding the word out according to the rules rather than trying to remember what can easily become a sight word with no clues at all.

We do something similar with vowels. In English, the schwa /ə/ is the most common vowel sound. This is the common sound of a vowel in an unstressed syllable, pronounced similar to a short *u* sound—/ŭ/.

Since this information is a bit over the head of the average five year old, we can explain it by describing these vowels as lazy. The word **alone** is listed in the spelling list like this:

a lone   Underline /ā/ to show that it's saying /ā/ at the end of a syllable. *O* says /ō/ because of the silent *e*. Double underline the silent *e*, and draw a bridge between the *o* and the *e*.

When we sound out the word, or "think to spell," we stress the /ā/ sound, but we can point out that it's a lazy vowel, so the child will hear people say /ə-lōn/.

It is important to stress all vowel sounds in the spelling lessons. Otherwise, depending on your accent, **pen** and **pin** might be indistinguishable.

Also, remember that analyzing words is merely a tool to help us understand spelling. Some words have multiple ways to analyze them. If you see a way to analyze a word that makes more sense to you and your child, use it.

top	Top. The first phonogram is /t/. [Wait while child writes it.] The next phonogram is /ŏ/, /ō/, /oo/. [Wait while child writes it.] The last phonogram is /p/. [Wait while child writes it.] /t/-/ŏ/-/p/. Top.
but	But. The first phonogram is /b/. The next phonogram is /ŭ/, /ū/, /ü/. The last phonogram is /t/. /b/-/ŭ/-/t/. But.
cat	Cat. The first phonogram is /c/, /s/. The next phonogram is /ă/, /ā/, /ä/. The last phonogram is /t/. /c/-/ă/-/t/. Cat.
red	Red. The first phonogram is /r/. The next phonogram is /ĕ/, /ē/. The last phonogram is /d/. /r/-/ĕ/-/d/. Red.
six	Six. The first phonogram is /s/, /z/. The next phonogram is /ĭ/, /ī/, /ē/, /y/. The last phonogram is /ks/. /s/-/ĭ/-/ks/. Six.
not	
hat	
bed	
ran	
run	

and

3
all — Put a small 3 above /ä/ to show that it's saying its third sound. We often double /l/ after a single vowel at the end of a base word.

3
tall — Put a small 3 above /ä/ to show that it's saying its third sound. We often double /l/ after a single vowel at the end of a base word.

am

b<u>e</u> — Underline /ē/; *e* says /ē/ at the end of a syllable.

<u>a</u> — Think to spell /ā/. Underline /ā/; *a* says /ā/ at the end of a syllable.

an

2
th<u>e</u> — Put a small 2 above /TH/ to show that it's saying its second sound. Underline /ē/; *e* says /ē/ at the end of a syllable.

2
is — Put a small 2 above /z/ to show that it's saying its second sound.

2
has — Put a small 2 above /z/ to show that it's saying its second sound.

add

We sometimes double a consonant after a single vowel at the end of a base word.

m<u>e</u>

Underline /ē/; *e* says /ē/ at the end of a syllable.

m<u>y</u>

Underline *y*. Vowel *y* says /ī/ at the end of a one-syllable base word.

mine͡

I says /ī/ because of the silent *e*; underline the silent *e* twice, and draw a bridge between the silent *e* and the *i*.

X
of

F sounds like /v/ in this word. Put a small X to show that it's an eXception.

g<u>o</u>

Underline /ō/; *o* says /ō/ at the end of a syllable.

do³

Put a small 3 above /oo/ to show that it's saying its third sound.

did

hit

step

1-D

bag

beg

big

bog

bug

can

s<u>o</u>   Underline /ō/; *o* says /ō/ at the end of a syllable.

n<u>o</u>   Underline /ō/; *o* says /ō/ at the end of a syllable.

pet

ten   Stress the /ĕ/ sound.

1-E

g<u>oo</u>d²	Underline the multi-letter phonogram(s). Put a small 2 above /ü/ to show that it's making its second sound.
fi<u>sh</u>	Underline the multi-letter phonogram(s).
last	
odd	We sometimes double a consonant after a single vowel at the end of a base word.
hill	We often double /l/ after a single vowel at the end of a base word.
in	
to³	Write a small 3 above /oo/ to show that it's making its third sound.
in to³	First syllable: in. Leave a small space between syllables. Second syllable: to. Write a small 3 above /oo/ to show that it's making its third sound. This is a compound word. That means that it's two words put together to become one word.
<u>ou</u>t	Underline the multi-letter phonogram(s).
on	

1-F

b<u>y</u>	Underline **y**. Vowel **y** says /ī/ at the end of a one-syllable base word.
up	
<u>o</u> v<u>er</u>	Underline /ō/ to show that it's saying /ō/ at the end of a syllable. Leave a small space before the second syllable. Use /er/ as in her. Underline the multi-letter phonogram(s).
at	
off	We often double /f/ at the end of a base word.
h<u>e</u>	Underline /ē/; **e** says /ē/ at the end of a syllable.
him	
hi²s	Put a small 2 above /z/ to show that it's saying its second sound.
<u>sh</u> <u>e</u>	Underline the multi-letter phonogram(s). Underline /ē/; **e** says /ē/ at the end of a syllable.
h<u>er</u>	Use /er/ as in her. Underline the multi-letter phonogram(s).

$\overset{3}{\text{y}\underline{\text{ou}}}$ Underline the multi-letter phonogram(s). Put a small 3 above /oo/ to show that it's saying its third sound. English words do not end in *u* or *i*, but "you" and "I" are special.

$\overset{3}{\text{y}\underline{\text{ou}}\text{r}}$ Underline the multi-letter phonogram(s). Put a small 3 above /oo/ to show that it's saying its third sound.

it

w<u>e</u> Underline /ē/; *e* says /ē/ at the end of a syllable.

us

<u>are</u> Underline the multi-letter phonogram(s).
$\underset{=5}{}$ Double underline the silent *e*.

wi<u>th</u> Underline the multi-letter phonogram(s).

b<u>ar</u>n Underline the multi-letter phonogram(s).

egg We sometimes double a consonant after a single vowel at the end of a base word.

hen

1-H

s<u>ay</u>	Underline the multi-letter phonogram(s).
s<u>ay</u>s ²	Think to spell /s-ā-z/. We sound out /sāz/, but we say /sĕz/. Underline the multi-letter phonogram(s). Put a small 2 above /z/ to show that it's saying its second sound.

s<u>ay</u>s — Think to spell /s-ā-z/. We sound out /sāz/, but we say /sĕz/. Underline the multi-letter phonogram(s). Put a small 2 above /z/ to show that it's saying its second sound.

s<u>ai</u>d — Think to spell /s-ā-d/. We sound out /sād/, but we say /sĕd/. Underline the multi-letter phonogram(s).

was (3 2) — Put a small 3 above /ä/ to show that it's saying its third sound. Put a small 2 above /z/ to show that it's saying its second sound.

w<u>e</u>re =5 — Use the /er/ in her. Underline the multi-letter phonogram(s). Double underline the silent *e*.

from

had

² <u>th</u>at — Underline the multi-letter phonogram(s). Put a small 2 above /TH/ to show that it's saying its second sound.

an <u>y</u> — Leave a small space between syllables. Underline *y*. Vowel *y* says /ē/ at the end of a multi-syllable word.

man <u>y</u> — Leave a small space between syllables. Underline *y*. Vowel *y* says /ē/ at the end of a multi-syllable word.

lone

O says /ō/ because of the silent **e**; underline the silent **e** twice, and draw a bridge between the silent **e** and the **o**.

a lone

Leave a small space between syllables. Underline /ā/ to show that it's saying /ā/ at the end of a syllable. **O** says /ō/ because of the silent **e**; underline the silent **e** twice, and draw a bridge between the silent **e** and the **o**.

one

Think to spell /ō-n/, but pronounce /won/. One used to rhyme with lone. Underline the silent **e** twice, and draw a bridge between the silent **e** and the **o**.

once
=3

Think to spell /ŏnse/. Once and one are exceptions. We say /w/, but there is no /w/ in the spelling. **C** says /s/ because of the silent **e**; underline the **c**, and double underline the silent **e**.

2
on ly

Leave a small space between syllables. Underline **y**. Vowel **y** says /ē/ at the end of a multi-syllable word.

pen

Stress the /ĕ/ sound.

nuts

sit

sat

cut

madę   *A* says /ā/ because of the silent *e*; underline the silent *e* twice, and draw a bridge between the silent *e* and the *a*.

makę   *A* says /ā/ because of the silent *e*; underline the silent *e* twice, and draw a bridge between the silent *e* and the *a*.

dog

ox

fox

keep   Underline the multi-letter phonogram(s).

feet   Underline the multi-letter phonogram(s).

see   Underline the multi-letter phonogram(s).

three   Underline the multi-letter phonogram(s).

tree   Underline the multi-letter phonogram(s).

<u>a</u> way	Leave a small space between syllables. Underline /ā/; *a* says /ā/ at the end of a syllable.
b<u>oy</u>	Underline the multi-letter phonogram(s).
din n<u>er</u>	User /er/ as in her.
³ ² fa <u>th</u> er	Leave a small space between syllables. Put a small 3 above /ä/ to show that it's saying its third sound. Use /er/ as in her. Underline the multi-letter phonogram(s). Put a small 2 above /TH/ to show that it's saying its second sound.
g<u>ar</u> den	Leave a small space between syllables.
find	*I* may say /ī/ when followed by two consonants.
kind	*I* may say /ī/ when followed by two consonants.
g<u>av</u><u>e</u>	*A* says /ā/ because of the silent *e*; underline the silent *e* twice, and draw a bridge between the silent *e* and the *a*. English words do not end in *v*; underline the *v*.
g<u>iv</u><u>e</u>₂	English words do not end in *v*; underline the *v*, and double underline the silent *e*.
g<u>ir</u>l	Use /er/ as in dirt.

8

1-L

house =5 — Underline the multi-letter phonogram(s). Double underline the silent *e*.

I — Underline /ī/; *i* says /ī/ at the end of a syllable. Definition: This is the word "I" that we use to speak about ourselves. We always write "I" with a capital letter. English words do not end in *u* or *i*, but "you" and "I" are special.

like — *I* says /ī/ because of the silent *e*; underline the silent *e* twice, and draw a bridge between the silent *e* and the *i*.

lit tle =4 — Every syllable must have a written vowel; double underline the silent *e*.

milk

moth er (²) — Leave a small space between syllables. Use /er/ as in her. Underline the multi-letter phonogram(s). Put a small 2 above /TH/ to show that it's saying its second sound.

nest

may — Underline the multi-letter phonogram(s).

play — Underline the multi-letter phonogram(s).

rain — Underline the multi-letter phonogram(s).

saw   Underline the multi-letter phonogram(s).

some   Double underline the silent *e*.
=5

time   *I* says /ī/ because of the silent *e*; underline the silent *e* twice, and draw a bridge between the silent *e* and the *i*.

some times   Leave a small space between syllables. At the end
=5   of the first syllable, double underline the silent *e*. In the second syllable, *i* says /ī/ because of the silent *e*; underline the silent *e* twice, and draw a bridge between the silent *e* and the *i*.

wet

for   Underline the multi-letter phonogram(s).

day   Underline the multi-letter phonogram(s).

af ter   Use /er/ as in her. Underline the multi-letter phonogram(s).

spot

what   Underline the multi-letter phonogram(s). Put a small 3 above /ä/ to show that it's saying its third sound.

will	We often double /l/ after a single vowel at the end of a base word.
²<u>th</u>em	Underline the multi-letter phonogram(s). Put a small 2 above /TH/ to show that it's saying its second sound.
²<u>th</u> ey	Underline the multi-letter phonogram(s). Put a small 2 above /TH/ to show that it's saying its second sound.
³t<u>w</u>o	Double underline the silent *w*. Put a small 3 above /oo/ to show that it's saying its third sound. Definition: the number two.
whit̂e	Underline the multi-letter phonogram(s). *I* says /ī/ because of the silent *e*; underline the silent *e* twice, and draw a bridge between the silent *e* and the *i*.
yes	
come	Double underline the silent *e*.
cam̂e	*A* says /ā/ because of the silent *e*; underline the silent *e* twice, and draw a bridge between the silent *e* and the *a*.
t<u>oo</u>	Underline the multi-letter phonogram(s). Definition: also.
went	

1-0

The **ed** ending shows that something happened in the past. It has three different sounds that it can make when we add it to the end of a base word.

melt

melt <u>ed</u>	Leave a small space between syllables. Underline the multi-letter phonogram(s).
r<u>ai</u>n<u>ed</u> [2 above ed]	Underline the multi-letter phonogram(s). Put a small 2 above /d/ to show that it's saying its second sound.
l<u>oo</u>k [2 above oo]	Underline the multi-letter phonogram(s). Put a small 2 above /ü/ to show that it's saying its second sound.
l<u>oo</u>k<u>ed</u> [2 above oo, 3 above ed]	Underline the multi-letter phonogram(s). Put a small 2 above /ü/ to show that it's saying its second sound. Put a small 3 above /t/ to show that it's saying its third sound.
ha<u>v</u><u>e</u> [=2]	English words do not end in **v**; underline the **v**, and double underline the silent **e**.
do<u>e</u>s [2 above es]	Double underline the silent **e**. Put a small 2 above /z/ to show that it's saying its second sound. Sound out /d-ŏ-z/. Say /d-ŭ-z/.
c<u>ou</u> l<u>d</u> [5 above ou]	Underline the multi-letter phonogram(s). Double underline the silent **l**.
w<u>ou</u> l<u>d</u> [5 above ou]	Underline the multi-letter phonogram(s). Double underline the silent **l**.
<u>sh</u> <u>ou</u> l<u>d</u> [5 above ou]	Underline the multi-letter phonogram(s). Double underline the silent **l**.

bye
‑‑=5

Underline **y**. Vowel **y** says /ī/ at the end of a one-syllable base word. Double underline the silent **e**. Definition: expresses leave-taking.

thing

Underline the multi-letter phonogram(s).

send

let ter

Leave a small space between syllables. Use /er/ as in her. Underline the multi-letter phonogram(s).

e ven

Leave a small space between syllables. Underline /ē/; **e** says /ē/ at the end of a syllable.

hope

O says /ō/ because of the silent **e**; underline the silent **e** twice, and draw a bridge between the silent **e** and the **o**.

to day
3

Leave a small space between syllables. Put a small 3 above /oo/ to show that it's saying its third sound. Underline the multi-letter phonogram(s). This is a compound word.

part

Underline the multi-letter phonogram(s).

park

Underline the multi-letter phonogram(s).

rule

U says /ū/ because of the silent **e**; underline the silent **e** twice, and draw a bridge between the silent **e** and the **u**.

1-Q

All the words in this list are contractions. "Contract" means to make smaller. A contraction is formed when we put two words together to make one shorter word. We leave some letters out, and we replace the missing letters with a punctuation mark called an apostrophe.

don't
The contraction for "do not." Put a small 2 above /ō/ to show that it's saying its second sound.

won't
The contraction for "will not." Put a small 2 above /ō/ to show that it's saying its second sound. [Note: The way this contraction is formed is irregular.]

did n't
Leave a small space between syllables. The contraction for "did not."

can't
The contraction for "cannot."

have n't
The contraction for "have not." Leave a small space between syllables. Remember, this is have + not. English words do not end in *v*; underline the *v*, and double underline the silent *e*.

I'm
The contraction for "I am." We always write the word "I" with a capital letter.

I'll
The contraction for "I will." We always write the word "I" with a capital letter.

it's
The contraction for "it is."

we'll
The contraction for "we will." Put a small 2 above /ē/ to show that it's saying its second sound.

th ey're
The contraction for "they are." Underline the multi-letter phonogram(s). Double underline the silent *e*.

<u>sh</u> eep	Underline the multi-letter phonogram(s).
baa	The sound a sheep makes.
pup p<u>y</u>	Leave a small space between syllables. Underline **y**. Vowel **y** says /ē/ at the end of a multi-syllable word.
b<u>ow</u>-w<u>ow</u>	The sound a puppy makes.
rab bit	Leave a small space between syllables.
<u>chick</u> en	Leave a small space between syllables. Underline the multi-letter phonogram(s).
clu<u>ck</u>	The sound a chicken makes.
c<u>ow</u>	Underline the multi-letter phonogram(s).
m<u>oo</u>	The sound a cow makes. Underline the multi-letter phonogram(s).
g<u>oa</u>t	Underline the multi-letter phonogram(s).

dove
=2

English words do not end in *v*; underline the *v*, and double underline the silent *e*.

coo

The sound a dove makes. Underline the multi-letter phonogram(s).

kit ten

Leave a small space between syllables.

mew

The sound a kitten makes. Underline the multi-letter phonogram(s).

tur key
(2)

Leave a small space between syllables. Put a small 2 above /ē/ to show that it's saying its second sound.

bird

Underline the multi-letter phonogram(s).

fly

Underline *y*. Vowel *y* says /ī/ at the end of a one-syllable base word.

flew

Underline the multi-letter phonogram(s).

mouse
=5

Underline the multi-letter phonogram(s). Double underline the silent *e*.

mice

I says /ī/ because of the silent *e*; underline the silent *e* twice, and draw a bridge between the silent *e* and the *i*. *C* says /s/ because of the silent *e*; underline the *c*.

r<u>oo</u>st <u>er</u>	Leave a small space between syllables. Underline the multi-letter phonogram(s).
² cr<u>ow</u>	Underline the multi-letter phonogram(s). Put a small 2 above /ō/ to show that it's saying its second sound.
g<u>oo</u>s<u>e</u> =5	Underline the multi-letter phonogram(s). Double underline the silent **e**.
g<u>ee</u>s<u>e</u> =5	Underline the multi-letter phonogram(s). Double underline the silent **e**.
<u>ow</u>l	Underline the multi-letter phonogram(s).
du<u>ck</u>	Underline the multi-letter phonogram(s).
qu<u>ack</u>	The sound a duck makes. Underline the multi-letter phonogram(s).
<u>chi</u>c<u>ks</u>	Underline the multi-letter phonogram(s).
<u>ch</u> <u>ir</u>p	The sound a chick makes. Underline the multi-letter phonogram(s).
pig	

black

gray

sleep

a̲ sl<u>ee</u>p   Underline /ā/; **a** says /ā/ at the end of a syllable.

dat<u>e</u>   **A** says /ā/ because of the silent **e**; underline the silent **e** twice, and draw a bridge between the silent **e** and the **a**.

2
f<u>our</u>

f<u>iv</u><u>e</u>   **I** says /ī/ because of the silent **e**; underline the silent **e** twice, and draw a bridge between the silent **e** and the **i**. English words do not end in **v**; underline the **v**.

nin<u>e</u>   **I** says /ī/ because of the silent **e**; underline the silent **e** twice, and draw a bridge between the silent **e** and the **i**.

sev en

<u>eigh</u>t

bas ket

guess — We often double /s/ after a single vowel at the end of a base word.

sing

2
sang

must

size — *I* says /ī/ because of the silent *e*; underline the silent *e* twice, and draw a bridge between the silent *e* and the *i*.

game — *A* says /ā/ because of the silent *e*; underline the silent *e* twice, and draw a bridge between the silent *e* and the *a*.

list

miss — We often double /s/ after a single vowel at the end of a base word.

cost

4

pret ty   Underline **y**. Vowel **y** says /ē/ at the end of a multi-syllable word.

blu̲e̲=2   Underline /ū/ to show that it's saying /ū/ at the end of a syllable. English words do not end in **u**; underline the silent **e** twice. Definition: the color blue.

2
t̲h̲e̲r̲e̲=5   [Note: Not the phonogram **er**, /ĕ-r/.] Double underline the silent **e**. Definition: that place or position.

sis te̲r̲

so̲o̲n

get

get ti̲n̲g̲

fo̲r̲ get   This is a compound word. That means that it's two words put together to become one word.

got

fo̲r̲ got   This is a compound word. That means that it's two words put together to become one word.

207

5

wi**ngs**

wi**sh**

3
want

2
w**oo**l

wa**rm**

h**or**se
=5
Double underline the silent *e*.

rid**es**
I says /ī/ because of the silent *e*; underline the silent *e* twice, and draw a bridge between the silent *e* and the *i*.

hap p**y**
Underline *y*. Vowel *y* says /ē/ at the end of a multi-syllable word.

r**ou**nd

a r**ou**nd
Underline /ā/; *a* says /ā/ at the end of a syllable.

6

where$_{=5}$	[Note: Not the phonogram *er*, /ĕ-r/.] Double underline the silent *e*.
Mr.	This is the title of respect for a man.
Mrs.	This is the title of respect for a married woman.
Miss	This is the title of respect for an unmarried woman.
jay	
land	
far	
how	
love$_{=2}$	English words do not end in *v*; underline the *v*, and double underline the silent *e*.
a bove$_{=2}$	Underline /ā/ to show that it's saying /ā/ at the end of a syllable. English words do not end in *v*; underline the *v*, and double underline the silent *e*.

7

ap ple=₄ Every syllable must have a written vowel; double underline the silent **e**.

morn ing

ˣ ³
who **Wh** says /h/. Put a small X to show that it's an eXception.

tell We often double /l/ after a single vowel at the end of a base word.

thank

farm

farm er

³
full We often double /l/ after a single vowel at the end of a base word.

bring

bod y Underline **y**. Vowel **y** says /ē/ at the end of a multi-syllable word.

m<u>ea</u>d <u>ow</u>
(with small 2's above "ea" and "ow")

mas t<u>er</u>

<u>lea</u> <u>v</u><u>e</u> (with =2) — English words do not end in *v*; underline the *v*, and double underline the silent *e*.

c<u>or</u>n

<u>o</u><u>h</u> — Underline /ō/ to show that it's saying /ō/ at the end of a syllable. Double underline the silent h.

tak<u>e</u> (with bridge) — **A** says /ā/ because of the silent *e*; underline the silent *e* twice, and draw a bridge between the silent *e* and the *a*.

hom<u>e</u> (with bridge) — **O** says /ō/ because of the silent *e*; underline the silent *e* twice, and draw a bridge between the silent *e* and the *o*.

th <u>ei</u>r

pl<u>ay</u> māt<u>e</u> (with bridge) — This is a compound word. **A** says /ā/ because of the silent *e*; underline the silent *e* twice, and draw a bridge between the silent *e* and the *a*.

fast

blow

horn

un der

wake — A says /ā/ because of the silent *e*; underline the silent *e* twice, and draw a bridge between the silent *e* and the *a*.

a wake — Underline /ā/; *a* says /ā/ at the end of a syllable. *A* says /ā/ because of the silent *e*; underline the silent *e* twice, and draw a bridge between the silent *e* and the *a*.

hay stack — This is a compound word.

ch ur ch

car

far

side — *I* says /ī/ because of the silent *e*; underline the silent *e* twice, and draw a bridge between the silent *e* and the *i*.

10

lost

tails

be hind   Underline /ē/; *e* says /ē/ at the end of a syllable.
            I may say /ī/ when followed by two consonants.

hear

page   *A* says /ā/ because of the silent *e*; underline
            the silent *e* twice, and draw a bridge between
            the silent *e* and the *a*. *G* says /j/ because of the
            silent *e*; underline the *g*.

night

sight

fight

right

light

sir

dame

A says /ā/ because of the silent **e**; underline the silent **e** twice, and draw a bridge between the silent **e** and the **a**.

live =2

English words do not end in **v**; underline the **v**, and double underline the silent **e**.

lane

A says /ā/ because of the silent **e**; underline the silent **e** twice, and draw a bridge between the silent **e** and the **a**.

coat

print

with in

This is a compound word.

rate

A says /ā/ because of the silent **e**; underline the silent **e** twice, and draw a bridge between the silent **e** and the **a**.

age

A says /ā/ because of the silent **e**; underline the silent **e** twice, and draw a bridge between the silent **e** and the **a**. **G** says /j/ because of the silent **e**; underline the **g**.

camp

d<u>ow</u>n

r<u>oa</u>d

w<u>ee</u>   Definition: small; it can also be the sound a
pig makes.

fl<u>ow</u> <u>er</u>s

<u>ea</u>t

stop

ba<u>ck</u>

cast

<u>sh</u>ip

<u>sh</u>ed

wig

woods

cracks

fill — We often double /l/ after a single vowel at the end of a base word.

flight

jail

file — *I* says /ī/ because of the silent *e*; underline the silent *e* twice, and draw a bridge between the silent *e* and the *i*.

club

case — *A* says /ā/ because of the silent *e*; underline the silent *e* twice, and draw a bridge between the silent *e* and the *a*.

soap

f<u>ou</u>nd

<u>e</u> y <u>e</u>
=–=5   Underline **y**. Vowel **y** says /ī/ at the end of a one-syllable base word. Double underline the silent **e** on each side.

<u>ea</u>rs   [Note: Not the phonogram **ear**, /ē-r/.]

h<u>ear</u>d

2
nos<u>e</u>   **O** says /ō/ because of the silent **e**; underline the silent **e** twice, and draw a bridge between the silent **e** and the **o**.

smell   We often double /l/ after a single vowel at the end of a base word.

m<u>ou</u> <u>th</u>

som<u>e</u> <u>thing</u>   This is a compound word. Double underline the
=5   silent **e**.

3
mo<u>ve</u>   English words do not end in **v**; underline the **v**,
=2   and double underline the silent **e**.

m<u>ea</u>n

n<u>ow</u>

cl<u>o</u> v<u>er</u>s   Underline /ō/; **o** says /ō/ at the end of a syllable.
  2
<u>th</u>en

f<u>i</u>x

c<u>ar</u>d

m<u>ai</u>l

f<u>ai</u>l

s<u>ai</u>l

b<u>oa</u>t

riv <u>er</u>

holệ

O says /ō/ because of the silent *e*; underline the silent *e* twice, and draw a bridge between the silent *e* and the *o*.

gro̲und

a̲ long

Underline /ā/; *a* says /ā/ at the end of a syllable.

3
flo̲or

re̲ al

Underline /ē/; *e* says /ē/ at the end of a syllable. Alternate way of marking with abnormal syllabification: re̲al

re̲ al ly̲

Underline /ē/; *e* says /ē/ at the end of a syllable. Alternate way of marking with abnormal syllabification: re̲al ly̲

bill

We often double /l/ after a single vowel at the end of a base word.

bu̲rn

tra̲in

bo̲rn

squ ir rel

com ing

br<u>ow</u>n

swept

2
cov <u>er</u> <u>ed</u>

next

win <u>ter</u>

<u>sh</u>ell

3
put

d<u>ea</u>r

We often double /l/ after a single vowel at the end of a base word.

18

c<u>ar</u>t

grand mo<u>th</u>²er   This is a compound word.

c<u>oo</u>²k <u>ie</u>²s

y<u>ar</u>d

br<u>ea</u>²d

at<u>e</u>   *A* says /ā/ because of the silent *e*; underline the silent *e* twice, and draw a bridge between the silent *e* and the *a*.

dra²nk

ex tra³

w<u>ea</u>²r

un til

19

nãme   **A** says /ā/ because of the silent **e**; underline the silent **e** twice, and draw a bridge between the silent **e** and the **a**.

²
took

³
al so   When all is a prefix, it loses an **l**. Underline /ō/; **o** says /ō/ at the end of a syllable.

²
low

³
to night

ch ain

spent

trust

dash

check

kit ty — Underline **y**. Vowel **y** says /ē/ at the end of a multi-syllable word.

land

un cle — Every syllable must have a written vowel; double underline the silent **e**.

aunt — This word can be pronounced either /ant/ or /änt/. Think to spell /änt/.

daugh ter

son

be came — Underline /ē/; **e** says /ē/ at the end of a syllable. **A** says /ā/ because of the silent **e**; underline the silent **e** twice, and draw a bridge between the silent **e** and the **a**.

dead

wrote — **O** says /ō/ because of the silent **e**; underline the silent **e** twice, and draw a bridge between the silent **e** and the **o**.

write — **I** says /ī/ because of the silent **e**; underline the silent **e** twice, and draw a bridge between the silent **e** and the **i**.

21

2
bro͟o͟k

both   ***O*** may say /ō/ when followed by two consonants.

tum ble͟   Every syllable must have a written vowel; double
=4   underline the silent ***e***.

still   We often double /l/ after a single vowel at the
              end of a base word.

whi͡le͟   ***I*** says /ī/ because of the silent ***e***; underline the
              silent ***e*** twice, and draw a bridge between the
              silent ***e*** and the ***i***.

loss   We often double /s/ after a single vowel at the
              end of a base word.

sto͡le͟   ***O*** says /ō/ because of the silent ***e***; underline
              the silent ***e*** twice, and draw a bridge between the
              silent ***e*** and the ***o***.

cop y͟   Underline ***y***. Vowel ***y*** says /ē/ at the end of a
              multi-syllable word.

de͟a͟l

kni͟t

wind mill   We often double /l/ after a single vowel at the
end of a base word.

³
wa t<u>er</u>

help

tr<u>u</u> l<u>y</u>   Underline /ū/; ***u*** says /ū/ at the end of a syllable.
Underline ***y***. Vowel ***y*** says /ē/ at the end of a
multi-syllable word.

its   Definition: shows that something belongs
to something.

t<u>o</u> tal   Underline /ō/; ***o*** says /ō/ at the end of a syllable.

<u>au</u> t<u>o</u>   Underline /ō/; ***o*** says /ō/ at the end of a syllable.

stamp

m<u>ay</u> b<u>e</u>   Underline /ē/; ***e*** says /ē/ at the end of a syllable.

s<u>ea</u>t

<u>nor</u> <u>th</u>

cold   ***O*** may say /ō/ when followed by two consonants.

let

2
sn<u>ow</u>

man

yet

tw<u>ee</u>t

2
yel l<u>ow</u>

<u>sh</u>all   We often double /l/ after a single vowel at the
end of a base word.

if

24

a bout   Underline /ā/; *a* says /ā/ at the end of a syllable.

pat ted

kn ow²

head²

hid

felt

ver y   [Note: Not the phonogram *er*; /ĕ-r/.]
          Underline *y*. Vowel *y* says /ē/ at the end of a
          multi-syllable word.

a gain   Underline /ā/; *a* says /ā/ at the end of a syllable.

as²

bee

up on   This is a compound word.

Christ mas   Double underline the silent *t*.

branch es

oth er

sleigh

jumped

high

best

lay

grew

Eas-t<u>er</u>

stopp<u>ed</u> ³

pl<u>ea</u>se ₂ ₌₅   Double underline the silent **e**.

t<u>oe</u>

cr<u>ee</u>p

f<u>ir</u>st

gr<u>ee</u>n

l<u>ea</u>p

pond

d<u>ee</u>p

po-ny   Underline /ō/; *o* says /ō/ at the end of a syllable.
Underline *y*. Vowel *y* says /ē/ at the end of a
multi-syllable word.

sick

gal lop ing

sad

ea ch

talk   Double underline the silent *l*.

maid

ros y   Underline *y*. Vowel *y* says /ē/ at the end of a
multi-syllable word.

ket tle   Every syllable must have a written vowel; double
underline the silent *e*.

fresh

doll

We often double /l/ after a single vowel at the end of a base word.

<u>ch</u> <u>ee</u>r

<u>sh</u>ut

<u>g</u>uest

<u>ea</u>s² <u>y</u>

Underline **y**. Vowel **y** says /ē/ at the end of a multi-syllable word.

just

c<u>oa</u> <u>ch</u>

ti<u>ck</u>

ta<u>ck</u>

box

d<u>ar</u>k

sl<u>ee</u>p y   Underline **y**. Vowel **y** says /ē/ at the end of a
<u> </u>   multi-syllable word.

t<u>ow</u>n

act

fact

mat <u>ter</u>

spend

post   *O* may say /ō/ when followed by two consonants.

elf

t<u>ore</u>
  =5   Double underline the silent *e*.

Elson

Primer

Story 1 Pre-Lesson

When you learned to write the letter **a**, you probably learned to write it like one of these:

a   *a*   *a*

In books, though, it is usually written like this:

a

The same thing happens with **g**. We write:

g   *g*   *g*

But in books, we read:

g

In this first story, there is a name which you have not yet studied. It is analyzed below. It's a proper name, so it begins with a capital letter. Can you sound it out? **C** says /s/ because of the silent **e**.

1. The Cat's Din-ner

Al-ice said, "Come, cat.

Come to din-ner."

The cat said, "No.

We will find a din-ner."

The cat saw a bird.

The kit-tens saw it, too.

The bird saw the cat.

It saw the kit-tens, too.

The bird flew a-way.

The cat said, "Come, kit-tens!

Come to the barn."

The cat went to the barn.

The kit-tens went, too.

The cat saw a mouse.

The mouse saw the cat.

The mouse ran a-way.

The cat went to the house.

The kit-tens went, too.

We said, "Come, cat, come!

Come, kit-tens, come!"

We gave them milk for din-ner.

Lillian M. Allen.

2. Spot's Kit-tens

Spot is my cat.

<u>Sh</u>e is bla<u>ck</u> and <u>wh</u>ite.

Come, Spot, come!

I like Spot.

Spot likes me.

Spot has four kit-tens.

One kit-ten is white.

One kit-ten is black.

I see a gray kit-ten, too.

One kit-ten is like Spot.

It is black and white.

One day it rained.

Spot was wet.

The kit-tens were wet, too.

Spot said, "Mew, mew!

We are wet! We are wet!"

Spot went in-to the house.

The kit-tens went, too.

They went to sleep.

Josephine Jarvis.

3. Al-ice and H<u>er</u> Kit-ten

Fa-<u>th er</u> s<u>ai</u>d, "Come, Al-ice.
Come to me.
S<u>ee</u> <u>the</u> bas-ket.
<u>Wh</u>at is in it?
Can y<u>ou</u> <u>g</u>uess?"

Al-ice: <u>Wh</u>at is in <u>the</u> bas-ket?

Fa-<u>th er</u>: Can y<u>ou</u> <u>g</u>uess?

Al-ice: Is it a b<u>ir</u>d?

Fa-th er: No, it is not a bird.

Al-ice: It is a lit-tle dog!

Fa-th er: No, it is not a dog.

Al-ice: Is it a kit-ten?

Fa-th er: Yes, it is a kit-ten.

Al-ice: Is it for me?

Fa-th er: Yes, it is for you.

The kit-ten is black.
Al-ice likes her kit-ten.
She gave it some milk.
The kit-ten likes milk.
Al-ice likes milk, too.
The kit-ten said, "Mew, mew!"
It went to sleep.

Jane L. Hoxie.

4. What Was in the Nest?

The girls saw a nest.

It was a lit-tle nest.

It was in a tree.

The girls saw two birds.

Can you see them?

They were pret-ty birds.

They were in the tree.

Moth-er bird sat on the nest.

One day she flew from the nest.

What was in the nest?

Can you guess?

The girls saw eggs in the nest.

They saw one, two, three, four eggs.

The four eggs were blue.

Moth-er bird sat on the nest.

She sat there day af-ter day.

One day she flew from the nest.

She sat in the tree.

She sang and sang.

Fa-th er bird sang, too.

The girls looked in the nest.

Can you guess what th ey saw?

Four lit-tle birds were in the nest.

Soon they could fly.

Moth-er bird said, "Fly, fly!"

Fa-ther bird said, "Fly, fly!"

They flew from the nest.

They flew from tree to tree.

One day they flew a-way.

The girls said, "Good-bye, good-bye!"

5. The White Dove

The dove flew to the barn.

It saw a white cow.

The dove said, "Coo, coo!

See my pret-ty wings!

Don't you wish you had wings?

You could fly and fly and fly."

The cow said, "Moo, moo!

I give milk to boys and girls.

Moo, moo! I don't want to fly!"

The dove flew to the sheep.
It said, "Coo, coo!
Don't you wish you had wings?
You could fly and fly and fly."

The sheep said, "Baa, baa!
I give wool to boys and girls.
The wool keeps them warm.
Baa, baa! I don't want to fly!"

The dove flew to the horse.
It said, "Coo, coo!
Don't you wish you had wings?
You could fly and fly and fly."

The horse said, "No, no!
I give rides to boys and girls.
No, no! I don't want to fly!"

The dove flew to the hen.

It said, "Coo, coo!

Don't you wish you could fly a-way?"

The hen said, "Cluck, cluck!

I give eggs to boys and girls.

I don't want to fly a-way."

"Coo, coo!" said the dove.

"Are you all hap-py?"

The cow said, "Moo, moo! Yes, yes!"

The sheep said, "Baa, baa! Yes, yes!"

The hen said, "Cluck, cluck! Yes, yes!"

The horse said, "Yes, yes!"

The dove said, "Coo, coo, coo!

I am hap-py, too."

She flew to her nest.

Harriet Warren.

6. The Jay and the Dove

Boy: Where do you come from, Mr. Jay?

Jay: From the land of play,
     From the land of play.

Boy: Where is that, Mr. Jay?

Jay: Far a-way. Far a-way.

Boy: Where do you come from,
    Mrs. Dove?

Dove: From the land of love,
    From the land of love.

Boy: How do you get there, Mrs. Dove?

Dove: Look a-bove. Look a-bove.

L. Alma-Tadema.

Story 7 Pre-Lesson

In this story, there is another name which you have not yet studied.
It is analyzed below. Remember that a proper name begins with a
capital letter. Can you sound it out?

Bob-b<u>ie</u>

7. Bob-bie and the Ap-ples

Bob-bie was a lit-tle boy.

His moth-er said, "I like ap-ples.

Can you get some for me?"

Bob-bie said, "Yes, Moth-er.

I will go to the ap-ple tree.

I will get some for you.

Good-bye, Moth-er, good-bye."

Bob-bie went to the ap-ple tree.

He looked and looked.

He could not see an-y ap-ples.

He said, "Good morn-ing, ap-ple tree.

Will you give me some ap-ples?"

The ap-ple tree said, "No, Bob-bie.

I have no ap-ples for you.

I gave my ap-ples a-way."

Bob-bie saw a cat.

He said, "I want some ap-ples.

I want them for Moth-er.

Who will give me some?

Can you tell me?"

The cat said, "Mew, mew, mew!

I have no ap-ples for you.

I want milk for din-ner.

Mew, mew, mew!"

The cat went to the house.

Bob-bie saw a dog.

He said, "Good morn-ing, dog.

I want some ap-ples for Moth-er.

Who will give me some?

Can you tell me?"

The dog said, "Bow-wow, bow-wow!

Go to the cow.

The cow will tell you."

Bob-bie said, "Thank you, dog."

Bob-bie ran to the cow.

He said, "Good morn-ing, cow.

I want some ap-ples for Moth-er.

Who will give me some?

Can you tell me?"

The cow said, "Moo, moo, moo!

I like ap-ples, too.

Go to the farm-er.

He has some ap-ples."

Bob-bie ran to the farm-er.

He said, "Good morn-ing, Mr. Farm-er.

Have you some ap-ples?

I want some for Moth-er."

The farm-er said, "Yes, lit-tle boy.

I will give you some ap-ples.

Come with me."

They went to the house.

Bob-bie saw a bag full of ap-ples.

He said, "May I have three ap-ples?

I want them for Moth-er."

The farm-er said, "Yes, lit-tle boy.

You may have four ap-ples.

One ap-ple is for you."

Bob-bie said, "Thank you, Mr. Farm-er.
I will give three to Moth-er."
A-way he ran to his moth-er.

Moth-er said, "What pret-ty ap-ples!
Did you bring them all for me?"
Bob-bie said, "I have four ap-ples.
Three are for you.
One is for me."

Moth-er said, "Thank you, Bob-bie.
Where did you get them?"

Bob-bie said, "I went to the farm-er.
The farm-er gave them to me."
Moth-er said, "You are a good boy."

Kate Whiting Patch, Adapted.

8. Al-ice and Her Moth-er

Moth-er said, "Come, Al-ice.

Sing lit-tle sis-ter to sleep."

Al-ice said, "I want to play.

I don't want to sing to sis-ter.

I want to play in the mead-ow.

The sheep plays there all day.

I want to play all day, too."

Moth-er said, "You may play all day.

You may go to the mead-ow."

Al-ice ran to the mead-ow.

She saw a sheep there.

Al-ice said, "Good morn-ing, sheep.

Will you play with me?

We can play all day."

The sheep said, "Baa, baa!

I can-not play all day.

I must get my din-ner.

I make wool for mas-ter.

I can-not play all day."

A dog was in the mead-ow.

Al-ice ran to the dog.

She said, "Good morn-ing, dog.

Will you play with me?

We can play all day."

The dog said, "Bow-wow!
I can-not play all day.
I must look af-ter the sheep.
I can-not leave them a-lone.
I can-not play all day."

A cow was in the mead-ow.
Al-ice ran to the cow.
She said, "Good morn-ing, cow.
Will you play with me?
We can play all day."

The cow said, "Moo, moo!
I can-not play all day.
I must find my din-ner.
I want to find some corn.
I give milk for your din-ner.
I can-not play all day."

A horse was in the mead-ow.

Al-ice ran to the horse.

She said, "Good morn-ing, horse.

Will you play with me?

We can play all day."

The horse said, "Oh, no!

I can-not play all day.

I give rides to boys and girls.

I take milk to your moth-er.

I can-not play all day."

Al-ice said, "I will go home.

No one will play with me."

Soon she came to a bird.

She said, "Good morn-ing, bird.

Will you play with me?

We can play all day."

The bird said, "No, thank you.

I must make my nest.

I can-not play all day."

Al-ice went home.

She saw her cat there.

She said, "Good morn-ing, Spot.

Will you play with me?

We can play all day."

Spot said, "No, thank you.

I must find a mouse.

My kit-tens must have their din-ner.

I can-not play all day."

Al-ice went to her moth-er.

She said, "Moth-er, I came home.

I could not find an-y play-mate.

No one could play all day.

I do not want to play all day.

I will sing sis-ter to sleep."

Al-ice sang and sang.

Soon lit-tle sis-ter was fast a-sleep.

9. Lit-tle Boy Blue

Lit-tle Boy Blue,

Come, blow your horn.

The sheep are in the mead-ow.

The cows are in the corn.

Where is the lit-tle boy

Who looks af-ter the sheep?

He is un-der the hay-stack,

Fast a-sleep.

Moth er Goose.

Where are you, Lit-tle Boy Blue?

Are you in the house?

Are you in the barn?

Are you in the mead-ow?

I see you, Lit-tle Boy Blue!

You are un-der the hay-stack.

Wake up! Wake up!

Blow your horn, Lit-tle Boy Blue!

Do you see your sheep?

They are in the mead-ow.

Where are your cows?

They are in the corn.

Blow your horn, Lit-tle Boy Blue!

Take the sheep and the cows

to the barn.

Story 10 Pre-Lesson

In this story, there is another name which you have not yet studied. It is analyzed below. Remember that a proper name begins with a capital letter. Can you sound it out? *O* says /ō/ at the end of a syllable.

Bo̲-pe̲e̲p

10. Lit-tle Bo-peep

Lit-tle Bo-peep
Has lost her sheep,
And can-not tell
Where to find them.
Leave them a-lone,
And they will come home,
And bring their tails
Be-hind them.

Moth er Goose.

Bo-peep: Good morn-ing, Boy Blue!
 I have lost my sheep.

Boy Blue: Have you looked for them?

Bo-peep: Yes, I have looked for them.

Boy Blue: Did you look in the corn?

Bo-peep: Yes. They were not there.

Boy Blue: Come with me to the mead-ow.
 We will look for them there.

Boy Blue: I hear your sheep, Bo-peep!
 I see them, too.

Bo-peep: Oh, yes! There th ey are!

They are in the mead-ow.

I will take them to the barn.

Boy Blue: I will go with you, Bo-peep.

Bo-peep: Thank you, Lit-tle Boy Blue.

Bring your horn with you.

11. Baa, Baa, Black Sheep

Baa, baa, Black Sheep,

Have you an-y wool?

Yes, sir! Yes, sir!

Three bags full.

One for my mas-ter.

One for my dame.

And one for the lit-tle boy

Who lives in the lane.

Mother Goose.

Girl: Good morn-ing, Black Sheep!
   Have you an-y wool?

Sheep: Yes! I have three bags full.

Girl: What will you do with it?

Sheep: One bag is for my mas-ter.
   One bag is for my dame.
   One bag is for Lit-tle Boy Blue.

Girl: Where is Lit-tle Boy Blue?

Sheep: He is in the lane.

Sheep: Good morn-ing, Boy Blue!
Guess what I have for you.

Boy: Is it a bag of wool?

Sheep: Yes, it is a bag of black wool.

Boy: Thank you, Black Sheep!
Thank you for the wool!
I will take it to moth-er.
She will make me a coat.
The coat will keep me warm.

12. The Pig's Din-ner

Lit-tle Pig went down the road.

He want-ed some din-ner.

Soon he came to a gar-den.

It was full of pret-ty flow-ers.

"Wee, wee!" said Lit-tle Pig.

"I want to go in-to that gar-den.

Flow-ers make a good din-ner."

He went in-to the gar-den.

Soon Red Hen came down the road.

Her lit-tle chick-ens were with her.

By and by they came to the gar-den

They saw the pret-ty flow-ers.

"Cluck, cluck!" said Red Hen.

"How pret-ty the flow-ers are!

Come with me in-to the gar-den.

We can find a good din-ner there."

They went in-to the gar-den to eat.

How hap-py they all were!

Soon White Cow came down the road.

She saw the pret-ty flow-ers.

She saw Lit-tle Pig in the gar-den.

She saw Red Hen and her chick-ens.

"Moo, moo!" she said.

"How pret-ty the flow-ers are!

They will make a good din-ner."

Red Hen said, "Cluck, cluck, come in!"

Lit-tle Pig said, "Wee, wee, come in!"

White Cow went in-to the gar-den.

Soon the farm-er came home.

He saw White Cow in the gar-den.

He saw Red Hen and her chick-ens.

He saw Lit-tle Pig, too.

"Stop eat-ing my flow-ers!" he said.

"Get out of my gar-den!"

A-way they all ran down the road!

"Good-bye, Mr. Farm-er!" said the hen.

"We had a good din-ner!" said the pig.

"We will come back soon!" said the cow.

Maud Lindsey.

Story 10 Pre-Lesson

In this story, there are two names which you have not yet studied. They are analyzed below. Remember that a proper name begins with a capital letter. Can you sound them out?

J<u>ac</u>k

Vowel *y* says /ē/ at the end of a multi-syllable word.

Pig-g<u>y</u>

13. Pig-gy Wig's House

Jack Rab-bit: Good morn-ing, Pig-gy
Wig! Where are you go-ing?

Pig-gy Wig: I am go-ing to the woods.
I want to make a house.

Jack Rab-bit: May I go with you?

Pig-gy Wig: What can you do?

Jack Rab-bit: I can cut down trees.
You can-not cut them down.

Pig-gy Wig: Come with me. I want you.

Gray Goose: Good morn-ing, Pig-gy Wig!
  Where are you go-ing?

Pig-gy Wig: I am go-ing to the woods.
  I want to make a house.

Gray Goose: May I go with you?

Pig-gy Wig: What can you do?

Gray Goose: Your house will have cracks.
  I can fill all the cracks.

Pig-gy Wig: Come with me. I want you.

Red Roos-ter: Good morn-ing,
  Pig-gy Wig!
  Where are you go-ing?

Pig-gy Wig: I am go-ing to the woods.
I want to make a house.

Red Roos-ter: May I go with you?

Pig-gy Wig: What can you do?

Red Roos-ter: I can wake you up.
I say, "Cock-a-doo-dle-doo!"

Pig-gy Wig: Come with me. I want you.

Soon they came to the woods.
Jack Rab-bit cut down the trees.
Pig-gy Wig made the house.
Gray Goose filled the cracks.
Red Roos-ter woke them up.
"Cock-a-doo-dle-doo!" he said.

14. The Lit-tle Pig

Once there was a lit-tle pig.
He lived with his moth-er in a pen.
One day he saw his four lit-tle feet.
"Wee, wee, Moth-er!" he said.
"See my four lit-tle feet!
What can I do with them?"

She said, "You can run with them."
The lit-tle pig ran and ran.
He ran round and round the pen.

One day he found his two lit-tle eyes,

"Wee, wee, Moth-er!" he said.

"See my two lit-tle eyes!

What can I do with them?"

She said, "You can see with them."

The lit-tle pig looked and looked.

He saw his moth-er.

He saw the cow.

He saw the sheep.

One day he found his two lit-tle ears.

"Wee, wee, Moth-er!" he said.

"See my two lit-tle ears!

What can I do with them?"

She said, "You can hear with them."

He heard the dog say, "Bow, wow!"

He heard the cat say, "Mew, mew!"

He heard the cow say, "Moo, moo!"

He heard the sheep say, "Baa, baa!"

One day he found his one lit-tle nose.

"Wee, wee, Moth-er!" he said.

"See my one lit-tle nose!

What can I do with it?"

She said, "You can smell with it.

Can you smell your din-ner?"

The lit-tle pig want-ed his din-ner.

He could not smell it.

"Wee, wee, wee!" he said.

Soon he found his one lit-tle mouth.

"Wee, wee, Moth-er!" he said.

"See my one lit-tle mouth!

What can I do with it?"

She said, "You can eat with it.

You can eat your din-ner."

The lit-tle pig want-ed his din-ner.
He could not find it.
"Wee, wee, wee!" he said.

Soon a girl came to the pen.
She had some-thing for Pig-gy.
Can you guess what it was?
The girl said, "Come, Pig-gy!
Come, Pig-gy, come!
I have some-thing for you.
It is some-thing good to eat."

What did the lit-tle pig hear
with his two lit-tle ears?

What did the lit-tle pig see
with his two lit-tle eyes?

What did the lit-tle pig do
with his four lit-tle feet?

What did the lit-tle pig smell
with his one lit-tle nose?

Guess what the lit-tle pig did
with his one lit-tle mouth.

15. Lit-tle Rab-bit

Stop, stop, Lit-tle Rab-bit!

Where are you go-ing?

Do not run a-way from me.

I can-not see you now.

Where are you, Lit-tle Rab-bit?

Oh, now I see you!

You are be-hind the flow-ers.

You are in the pret-ty clo-vers.

Stop, stop, Lit-tle Rab-bit!

Do not eat the clo-vers.

They are so pret-ty.

They are so white.

They are white like your ears.

The clo-vers are so lit-tle, now.

Soon they will be big.

Then you may eat them.

Good-bye, Lit-tle Rab-bit, good-bye!

16. Jack Rab-bit's Vis-it

Fa-th er Squir-rel lived in a tree.

His home was a hole in the tree.

Moth-er Squir-rel lived there, too.

Three lit-tle squir-rels lived with them.

Th ey were pret-ty lit-tle squir-rels.

Th ey had big eyes and big tails.

Th ey played in the trees.

Th ey played on the ground, too.

One day th ey we re all at home.

Th ey we re eat-ing nuts.

Jack Rab-bit came a-long.

He said, "May I come in?"

"Yes, come in," said Fa-th er Squir-rel.

Jack Rab-bit came in-to the house.

"Sit down," said Moth-er Squir-rel.

He sat down on the floor.

A lit-tle squir-rel said, "Eat some nuts!"

"No, thank you," said Jack Rab-bit.

"I do not like nuts, Lit-tle Squir-rel."

Squir-rel: Rab-bit, where do you live?

Rab-bit: I live in the ground.
   I have a warm hole there.

Squir-rel: What do you eat?

Rab-bit: Oh, I eat leaves.
   What do you eat, Squir-rel?

Squir-rel: We eat nuts.
   Will you live with us?

Rab-bit: No! I can-not live in a tree.
   I must go now. Good-bye!

Mary Dendy.

17. Bob-bie Squir-rel's Tail

See Bob-bie Squir-rel.

What a big tail he has!

One day he ran down a tree.

Jack Rab-bit was com-ing a-long.

His tail was lit-tle.

Jack Rab-bit said, "Look at Bob-bie!

He wants us to see his big tail."

Brown Owl said, "Oh, see Bob-bie!

He has his tail a-bove his back."

Bob-bie Squir-rel ran to a nut tree.

There were nuts un-der the tree.

Bob-bie made a hole in the ground.

It was a big round hole.

He swept the nuts in-to it.

He swept them with his big tail.

Bob-bie cov-er ed them with leaves.

He swept the leaves with his tail, too.

Then he ran to his home in the tree.

He will eat the nuts next win-ter.

Guess what Bob-bie found at home!

He found shells on the floor!

A lit-tle squir-rel had put them there.

"Oh, dear me!" said Bob-bie.

"The floor must be swept!"

So Bob-bie swept the floor.

He swept it with his big tail.

By and by night came.

Bob-bie went to sleep on the floor.

Guess what he did with his tail!

Carolyn S. Bailey.

Story 18 Pre-Lesson

In this story, there is a name which you have not yet studied. It is analyzed below. Remember that a proper name begins with a capital letter. Can you sound it out?

Ned

18. Ned Vis-its Grand-moth-er

Ned had a lit-tle red cart.

He want-ed Grand-moth-er to see it.

His moth-er gave him a big ap-ple.

She gave him some cook-ies, too.

He put the ap-ple and the cook-ies in-to
the cart.

Then he went to see Grand-moth-er.

Soon Ned came to a mead-ow.

He saw Lit-tle Pig there.

"Good morn-ing!" said Ned.

Lit-tle Pig said, "Wee, wee!
I want some cook-ies."
Ned said, "No, no, Lit-tle Pig!
They are for Grand-moth-er.
Come with me to her house.
She will give you some din-ner."
So Lit-tle Pig went a-long with Ned.

Soon they came to a barn.
Ned saw White Hen.
"Good morn-ing!" said Ned.
White Hen said, "Cluck, cluck!
I want some cook-ies."
Ned said, "No, no, White Hen!
They are for Grand-moth-er.
Come with us to her house.
She will give you some din-ner."
So White Hen went a-long with them.

Soon they came to a house.

Gray Kit-ten was in the yard.

"Good morn-ing!" said Ned.

Gray Kit-ten said, "Mew, mew!

I want some cook-ies."

Ned said, "No, no, Gray Kit-ten!

They are for Grand-moth-er.

Come with us to her house.

She will give you some din-ner."

So Gray Kit-ten went a-long with them.

Soon they came to a big tree.

Lit-tle Bird was in the tree.

He flew down to the ground.

"Good morn-ing!" said Ned.

Lit-tle Bird said, "Peep, peep!

I want some cook-ies."

Ned said, "No, no, Lit-tle Bird!

They are for Grand-moth-er.

Come with us to her house.

She will give you some din-ner."

So Lit-tle Bird went a-long with them.

Grand-moth-er looked down the road.

"What do I see?" she said.

"Oh, it is lit-tle Ned!

Good morn-ing, Ned!"

Ned said, "Good morn-ing!

See my red cart, Grand-moth-er!

I have some cook-ies for you.

I have a big ap-ple for you, too."

Grand-moth-er said, "Thank you, Ned!

I like cook-ies and ap-ples."

Grand-moth-er: Ned, what can I give you?

Ned: Oh, give us some din-ner!

Grand-moth-er: What do you like, Ned?

Ned: Lit-tle Pig likes corn.

    White Hen likes corn, too.

    Lit-tle Bird likes bread.

    Gray Kit-ten likes milk.

    I like milk, too.

Grand-moth-er: I will get corn and bread.

    I will get milk, too.

Lit-tle Bird ate bread.

White Hen and Lit-tle Pig ate corn.

Ned and Gray Kit-ten drank milk.

Grand-moth-er ate the cook-ies.

She ate the ap-ple, too.

Ned said, "We must go now.

Thank you for the good din-ner."

"Good-bye, Ned," said Grand-moth-er.

"Good-bye, Grand-moth-er," said Ned.

Soon they came to the big tree.

"Good-bye, Lit-tle Bird," said Ned.

"Peep, peep!" said Lit-tle Bird.

Next they came to the house.

"Good-bye, Gray Kit-ten!" said Ned.

"Mew, mew!" said Gray Kit-ten.

Next they came to the barn.

"Good-bye, White Hen!" said Ned.

"Cluck, cluck!" said White Hen.

Next they came to the mead-ow.

"Good-bye, Lit-tle Pig!" said Ned.

"Wee, wee!" said Lit-tle Pig.

Ned ran to his moth-er.

Marion Wathen.

19. Lit-tle Owl

Lit-tle Owl lived with Moth-er Owl.

One night Moth-er Owl said, "Wh oo!

Big owls say 'Wh oo, wh oo!'

You must say 'Wh oo, wh oo.'"

Lit-tle Owl said, "Oh, no, Moth-er!

I don't want to say 'Wh oo, wh oo.'"

Moth-er Owl said, "You must say 'Wh oo.'

The boy and the cat will hear you.

They will run a-way from you."

Lit-tle Owl would not say "Wh oo."

Moth-er Owl said, "A cat will get you!"

Lit-tle Owl said, "What is a cat?"

Moth-er Owl said, "A cat has big eyes.

It can see at night.

It eats birds."

Lit-tle Owl said, "What do cats say?

Do cats say 'Wh oo, wh oo,' Moth-er?"

"No, no!" said Moth-er Owl.

"Cats say 'Mew, mew!'"

"Moth-er, Moth-er!" said Lit-tle Owl.

"I want to see a cat!

I want to hear her say, 'Mew, mew!'"

Moth-er Owl said, "You must say 'Wh oo.'

You are not a good lit-tle owl."

One day Moth-er Owl flew a-way.

Lit-tle Owl sat in a tree.

"Mew, mew!" he said. "Mew, mew!"

A cat heard him say, "Mew, mew!"

She said, "Lit-tle Owl, Lit-tle Owl!

Can you eat a mouse?"

"Oh, yes!" said Lit-tle Owl.

The cat said, "Do you eat birds?"

"Oh, no! I am a bird," said Lit-tle Owl.

The cat said, "I eat birds.

I will eat you, Lit-tle Owl!"

A boy came to the tree.

His name was Bob-bie.

He was a kind lit-tle boy.

He saw Lit-tle Owl and the cat.

Bob-bie said, "Cat, go a-way!

You must not eat Lit-tle Owl!
I want to take him home with me.
I want to give him some din-ner.
Good-bye, Cat, good-bye!"
So Bob-bie took Lit-tle Owl home
with him.

Lit-tle Owl was not hap-py.
He want-ed to go to his moth-er.
That night Moth-er Owl came to him.
Lit-tle Owl said, "Moth-er, Moth-er!
I will be a good lit-tle owl.
I will say 'Wh oo, wh oo!'
Take me home with you."
Moth-er Owl said, "No, no, Lit-tle Owl!
I can-not take you with me."
In the morn-ing she flew a-way.

Lit-tle Owl would not eat his din-ner.

All day he said, "Wh oo, wh oo!"

Bob-bie's moth-er heard Lit-tle Owl.

She said, "Bob-bie, hear Lit-tle Owl!

He wants to go to his moth-er.

Take him to his home."

Bob-bie took Lit-tle Owl to the woods.

"Moth-er Owl! Moth-er Owl!" he said.

"Do you want Lit-tle Owl?"

Moth-er Owl said, "Wh oo, wh oo!"

Lit-tle Owl said, "Wh oo, wh oo," too.

Bob-bie gave Lit-tle Owl to his moth-er.

How hap-py th ey all were!

Anne Schütze.

20. What Brown Kit-ty Saw

Once Gray Kit-ty sat in a tree.

Brown Kit-ty sat on the ground.

Gray Kit-ty looked at Brown Kit-ty.

Brown Kit-ty looked at Gray Kit-ty.

"Good morn-ing," said Gray Kit-ty.

"Mew, mew," said Brown Kit-ty.

"What a pret-ty coat you have!"

Brown Kit-ty ran a-way.

Gray Kit-ty looked at her.

She said, "See Brown Kit-ty run!

I wish I could run, too."

Brown Kit-ty ran to her home.

Guess what she said to her moth-er!

She said,

    "A lit-tle gray kit-ten

    Sat in a tree!

    I looked at her,

    She looked at me!"

Kate L. Brown.

Story 21 Pre-Lesson

In this poem, there is a little nonsense song that a child is singing.
Can you sound it out?

3   **3**

Ti-ri-li, ti-ri-li,

Ting, ting, ting

21. The Brook

Brook, brook, come a-long.
Run a-long with me!
Oh, what hap-py play-mates
You and I will be!

You can run, I can run.
Both of us can sing,
Ti-ri-li, ti-ri-li,
Ting, ting, ting!

Brook, brook, come a-long.
Run a-long with me!
Oh, dear me, I tum-bled in!
What a sight to see!

You are wet, I am wet.
Still we both can sing,
Ti-ri-li, ti-ri-li,
Ting, ting, ting

Laura E. Richards.

22. The Wind-mill

Once there was a big wind-mill.

It went round and round.

It gave wa-ter to the hors-es and

the cows.

It gave wa-ter to the sheep, too.

One day it said, "I will stop!

I will not go round and round."

So the wind-mill was still all day.

By and by the wind came.

It said, "I will help you, Wind-mill.

I will make you go round and round
and round."

"No, no!" said the wind-mill.
"I don't want to go round and round
and round.
I don't want you to help me.
I want to be still all day."
The wind said, "You must go round!
The hors-es and cows want wa-ter.
I will blow for you."
The wind-mill would not go.
It would not bring an-y wa-ter.
So the wind went a-way.

By and by the hors-es came home.
They had helped the farm-er all day.
The cows and the sheep came, too.
They all ran to the wind-mill.

They all want-ed some wa-ter.

There was no wa-ter for them!

They said, "Oh, Wind-mill!

Will you be kind to us?

Will you give us wa-ter, Wind-mill?"

The wind-mill was not hap-py.

It said, "There is no wa-ter.

Wind, come and help me."

The wind came at once.

"I will blow for you," it said.

The wind-mill went round and round.

Soon the wa-ter came.

The hors-es drank and drank.

The cows and the sheep drank, too.

How hap-py the wind-mill was!

Kathlyn Libbey.

23. Who Likes North Wind?

"Oo-oo! Oo-oo!" said North Wind.

Lit-tle Bird sat in a tree.

He want-ed to keep warm.

"Peep, peep! Peep, peep!" he said.

"How cold the wind is!

Win-ter is com-ing.

I must fly a-way. Good-bye!"

"Oo-oo! Oo-oo!" said North Wind.

Gray Squir-rel sat on the ground.

"How cold the wind is!" he said.

"Win-ter is com-ing.

There are nuts in the woods.

I will fill my nest with nuts.

I can eat them in the win-ter.

My nest will keep me warm.

I will go to my home in the tree."

"Oo oo! Oo-oo!" said North Wind.

Black Kit-ten was in the yard.

"Mew, mew, mew!" he said.

"How cold the wind is!

Win-ter is com-ing.

I want to go in-to the house.

I can keep warm there.

I can get some milk there, too.

I can sleep on the warm floor.

Mew, mew! Mew, mew!

Let me come in-to the house!"

"Oo oo! Oo-oo!" said North Wind.

Jack ran to the barn.

"Hur-rah! Hur-rah!" he said.

"How cold the wind is!

Win-ter is com-ing.

It is go-ing to snow.

I will make a snow man.

I will ride down the hill, too.

Hur-rah! Hur-rah! Hur-rah!"

"Oo-oo! Oo-oo!" said North Wind.

"How hap-py I am now!

I have found a play-mate.

Oo-oo, Jack, oo-oo!

The white snow is com-ing.

See! It is com-ing now!

You and I will be play-mates.

How hap-py we will be!

Oo-oo, Jack, oo-oo!"

Folk Tale.

Story 24 Pre-Lesson

In this story, there is a name which you have not yet studied. It is analyzed below. Remember that a proper name begins with a capital letter. Can you sound it out? Vowel *y* says /ē/ at the end of a multi-syllable word.

Pat-ty

24. How Pat-ty Gave Thanks

Cow: Good morn-ing to you all!
　　　I have some-thing to tell you.
　　　Can you guess what it is?

Horse: Is it a-bout a lit-tle girl?

Cow: Yes! It is a-bout a lit-tle girl.
　　　Can you guess who she is?

Sheep: Is it some-thing a-bout Pat-ty?

Cow: Yes! It is a-bout Pat-ty.

Horse: I want to hear a-bout Pat-ty.
　　　We all love Pat-ty.

Sheep: Yes! Tell us a-bout Pat-ty.

Cow: What a good girl Pat-ty is!
    She came to me this morn-ing.
    She said, "Good morn-ing, Cow!
    This is Thank-you day.
    You give me milk.
    I like your good milk.
    Thank you, Cow, thank you!"
    She gave me a big ap-ple.
    I like to give milk to Pat-ty.

Sheep: Bob, did you see Pat-ty?

Horse: Yes, Pat-ty came to me, too.
    She said, "You dear horse!
    You give me rides.
    Thank you, Bob, thank you!"
    She pat-ted me and pat-ted me.

Then she gave me some hay.
I will give her a ride soon.

Cow: How kind Pat-ty is!
Bob likes to give her rides.
I like to give her milk.

Horse: Did Pat-ty thank you, Sheep?

Sheep: Yes, she came to us, too.
She said, "Good morn-ing!
I know what you give me.
You give me wool.
The wool keeps me warm.
Thank you, thank you!"
Then she gave us some wa-ter.

Cow: How kind Pat-ty is!
Bob likes to give her rides.

Sheep like to give her wool.
I like to give her milk.

Cow: Did Pat-ty thank the hens, too?

Horse: Yes! I heard her thank them.
Then she gave them some corn.

Sheep: What do the hens give Pat-ty?

Cow: They give her eggs.

Horse: She said "Thank you" to us all.

Cow: How kind Pat-ty is!
Bob likes to give her rides.
Sheep like to give her wool.
Hens like to give her eggs.
I like to give her milk.

Emilie Poulsson.

25. The Lit-tle Christ-mas Tree

Once there were three trees.

They lived on a hill.

One tree was big.

One tree was not so big.

One tree was lit-tle.

The snow came down up-on them.

They said, "Christ-mas is com-ing!

We want to be Christ-mas trees!"

A lit-tle bird came a-long.

The lit-tle bird was lost.

He could not find his moth-er.

He went to the big tree.

"Are you a kind tree?" he said.

"May I sit in your branch-es?

The snow is so cold!"

The big tree said, "No, no!

I don't want birds in my branch-es.

I am go-ing to be a Christ-mas tree!"

"How cold I am!" said the bird.

"I wish I could find a kind tree!

It would keep me warm."

He went on up the hill.

Soon he came to the next tree.

"Are you a kind tree?" he said.
"May I sit in your branch-es?
The snow is so cold!
I am lost, dear Tree.
I can-not find my moth-er."

Now the tree was not kind.
It was like the big tree.
It said, "No, Lit-tle Bird, no!
I don't want birds in my branch-es.
I am go-ing to be a Christ-mas tree!"

"How cold I am!" said the bird.
"I wish I could find a kind tree!"
He went on up the hill.
Soon he came to the lit-tle tree.

He said, "Lit-tle Tree, I am lost!
May I sit in your warm branch-es?
The snow is so cold!"
Now the lit-tle tree was kind.
It was not like the oth-er trees.
It said, "Oh, yes, dear Bird!
You may sit in my branch-es."
How hap-py the lit-tle bird was!

By and by the bird heard some-thing.
A sleigh was com-ing up the hill!
It did not stop at the big tree.
It did not stop at the next tree.
On it went to the lit-tle tree.
"It has come to us!" said the bird.
A man jumped out of the sleigh.
Can you guess who he was?

"What a pret-ty tree!" said the man.

"I want it for a Christ-mas tree."

So he took it with him in the sleigh.

He took the little bird, too.

He said, "I will take you to Pat-ty.

She will keep you warm."

A-way they all flew in the sleigh.

How hap-py the lit-tle tree was!

How hap-py the lit-tle bird was!

Mary McDowell.

Story 26 Pre-Lesson

In this story, there are two names which you have not yet studied. They are analyzed below. Remember that a proper name begins with a capital letter. Can you sound them out? These two names rhyme. That means that they end with the same sound.

Ra<u>y</u>

Ma<u>y</u>

26. The Eas-ter Rab-bit

Lit-tle Rab-bit sat by the road.

Ray and May came a-long.

They did not see Lit-tle Rab-bit.

"Eas-ter is com-ing soon," said May.

"Let us make a nest in the yard.

The Eas-ter Rab-bit will see it.

He will leave pret-ty eggs in it for us."

Ray said, "Yes, let us make a nest!"

A-way they ran to make the nest.

Lit-tle Rab-bit ran to his moth-er.

"I want to be the Eas-ter Rab-bit,"
he said.

"What is the Eas-ter Rab-bit?"
said his moth-er.

"The Eas-ter Rab-bit puts eggs
in-to nests," he said.

"Ray and May are go-ing to make
a nest in the yard.

I want to put eggs in-to it."

His moth-er said, "Do not go a-way!

Ray and May will get you."

Moth-er Rab-bit went to the gar-den.

Then Lit-tle Rab-bit ran a-way.

He want-ed to find Eas-ter eggs.

Ray and May saw Lit-tle Rab-bit.

They ran af-ter him.

"Stop, Lit-tle Rab-bit!" said Ray.

"Stop! We want you.

Oh, now we have you!

We will keep you in the barn."

They took Lit-tle Rab-bit to the barn.

They pat-ted him and pat-ted him.

They gave him leaves for din-ner.

Lit-tle Rab-bit want-ed his moth-er.

Ray said, "The rab-bit is not hap-py.

Let us take him to the yard.

He will put Eas-ter eggs in-to the nest!"

They took Lit-tle Rab-bit to the yard.

A-way he ran down the road!

By and by Lit-tle Rab-bit stopped.

He said, "I will go back to the yard.

I want to make Ray and May hap-py.

I want to be the Eas-ter Rab-bit.

I will look for eggs in the yard."

Lit-tle Rab-bit ran back to the yard.

He could not find an-y eggs there.

Then he looked in the nest.

Can you guess what he saw?

He saw two lit-tle kit-tens!

One kit-ten was white.

The oth-er kit-ten was black.

Then he saw the moth-er cat.

She had a gray kit-ten in her mouth.

She put it in-to the nest, too.

Soon May came to the nest.

She was looking for Eas-ter eggs.

"Oh, see the kit-tens!" she said.

"Come, Ray! See what is in the nest!"

Ray ran to look in the nest.

"What pret-ty kit-tens!" he said.

How hap-py Ray and May were!

Lit-tle Rab-bit was hap-py, too.

"The cat is the Eas-ter Rab-bit!" he said.

Then he ran home to his moth-er.

Anne Schütze.

Our Flag

I kn ow three lit-tle sis-ters.

You kn ow the sis-ters, too.

For one is red, and one is white,

The oth-er one is blue.

Hur-rah for the three lit-tle sis-ters!

Hur-rah for the red, white, and blue!

Hur-rah! Hur-rah! Hur-rah! Hur-rah!

Hur-rah for the red, white, and blue.

E. L. McCord.

27. In the Barn Yard

Once there was a big barn yard.

White Cow and Pig-gy Wig lived in it.

Red Hen and Gray Po-ny lived there, too.

Pig-gy Wig said, "Wee, wee!

What a good day to eat and sleep!"

Red Hen said, "Cluck, cluck!

What a good day to go to the gar-den!"

White Cow said, "Moo, moo!

What a good day to eat hay!"

Gray Po-ny said, "Good morn-ing!

What a good day to give rides!"

Pig-gy Wig said, "Wee, wee!

I want to eat and sleep.

I don't want to give rides."

Red Hen said, "Cluck, cluck!

I want to go to the gar-den.

I don't want to give rides."

White Cow said, "Moo, moo!

I want to go to the mead-ow.

I want to eat hay there.

I don't want to give rides,"

Gray Po-ny said, "I want to run.

I want to give mas-ter a ride."

The mas-ter came to the barn yard.

He said, "Pig-gy Wig, eat your din-ner.

You may eat and sleep all day.

Red Hen, go to the gar-den.

You will find some-thing to eat there.

White Cow, go to the mead-ow.
You will find hay there.
Gray Po-ny, come to me.
We will go to see a sick girl.
She lives far, far a-way."

The mas-ter jumped up-on Gray Po-ny.
A-way they went gal-lop-ing, gal-lop-ing,
gal-lop-ing.
By and by they came to the home of the
sick girl.
The mas-ter went in-to the house.
Soon he came back to Gray Po-ny.

He said, "We helped the sick girl.
She can go out to play soon.
You are a good po-ny."
How hap-py Gray Po-ny was!
The mas-ter jumped up-on Gray Po-ny.

He said, "Now we will go home."
A-way they went gal-lop-ing back
to the barn yard.

Red Hen said, "Cluck, cluck, Gray Po-ny!
I ate corn in the gar-den."
White Cow said, "Moo, moo!
What a good day I have had!
I ate hay in the mead-ow."
Pig-gy Wig said, "Wee, wee!
What a good sleep I have had!
I had a good din-ner, too."
Gray Po-ny said, "How hap-py I am!
I have had a good day, too.
I helped the lit-tle girl."

Frances Weld Danielson.

28. Al-ice and the Bird

Al-ice was fast a-sleep.

A bird saw her.

"Wake up! Wake up!" sang the bird.

"Wake up, Lit-tle Girl!" it sang.

Al-ice woke up!

She jumped out of her bed.

She saw the bird in the tree.

Al-ice went to play with Pat-ty.

She took her doll with her.

Pat-ty said, "I want the doll!"

Al-ice said, "No, I want it!"

"Give up! Give up!" sang the bird.

Al-ice looked up in-to the tree.

There sat the bird!

"Give up! Give up!" it sang.

"I hear you, Lit-tle Bird," said Al-ice.

"I will give up! I will give up!

Pat-ty, you may have the doll."

Al-ice went home to din-ner.

Her moth-er was not there.

"Oh, where is moth-er?" she said.

"I want my din-ner!"

"Cheer up! Cheer up!" sang the bird

Al-ice looked up in-to the tree.

There sat the bird!

"Cheer up! Cheer up!" it sang.

"I will cheer up," said Al-ice.

"I will cheer up and be hap-py."

She ran to play with her kit-ten.

She sang and was hap-py.

Af-ter din-ner, Al-ice went for a ride.

Then her moth-er put her to bed.

Her black eyes would not shut.

"Shut them up!" sang the bird.

"Shut them up! Shut them up!"

"I will shut them up," said Al-ice.

Soon she was fast a-sleep.

How hap-py the bird was!

It had helped Al-ice all the day.

Emily Rose Burt.

Story 29 Pre-Lesson

In this story, there are two names which you have not yet studied. They are analyzed below. Remember that a proper name begins with a capital letter. Can you sound them out?

Nid-d<u>y</u>

Nod-d<u>y</u>

29. Dark Po-ny

Once there was a po-ny.

His name was Dark.

He took boys and girls to Sleep-y Town.

One night a boy stopped him.

The boy's name was Nod-dy.

Nod-dy said,

"Take me down

To Sleep-y Town!"

Nod-dy jumped up-on Dark Po-ny.

A-way th ey went gal-lop-ing,

gal-lop-ing, gal-lop-ing.

Soon th ey came to a lit-tle girl.

The girl's name was Nid-dy.

Nid-dy said,

"Let me go, too,

Take me with you!"

Dark Po-ny stopped gal-lop-ing.

Nod-dy said, "We will take you."

Nid-dy jumped up be-hind Nod-dy.

"Go, go, Dark Po-ny!" she said.

A-way th ey went gal-lop-ing,

gal-lop-ing, gal-lop-ing.

Soon th ey came to a white dog.

The dog said,

"Bow, wow, wow!

Take me now!"

Dark Po-ny stopped gal-lop-ing.

Nod-dy jumped down to get the dog.

Then he jumped up-on the po-ny.

"Go, go, Dark Po-ny!" he said.
A-way they went gal-lop-ing,
gal-lop-ing, gal-lop-ing.

Soon they came to a black cat.
The cat said,
"Mew, mew, mew!
Take me, too!"
Dark Po-ny stopped gal-lop-ing.
Nid-dy jumped down to get the cat.
Then she jumped up-on the po-ny.
She took the cat with her.
"Go, go, Dark Po-ny!" she said.
A-way they went gal-lop-ing,
gal-lop-ing, gal-lop-ing.

By and by they came to a barn.
They saw a red roos-ter there.
The red roos-ter said,

"Cock-a-doo-dle-doo!

Take me, too!"

Dark Po-ny stopped gal-lop-ing.

Nid-dy said, "Come, Red Roos-ter!

You may sit be-hind me."

The red roos-ter flew up be-hind Nid-dy.

"Go, go, Dark Po-ny!" said Nid-dy.

A-way they went gal-lop-ing,

gal-lop-ing, gal-lop-ing.

Soon they came to the woods.

They saw a gray squir-rel there.

The squir-rel said,

"Take me, too,

A-long with you!"

Nid-dy said, "Yes, Gray Squir-rel.

We will take you.

Sit by the red roos-ter."

The squir-rel sat by the red roos-ter.
"Go, go, Dark Po-ny!" said Nid-dy.
A-way they went gal-lop-ing,
gal-lop-ing, gal-lop-ing.

They went gal-lop-ing on and on.
How hap-py they all were!
They sang and sang and sang.
By and by Dark Po-ny stopped.
He had come to Sleep-y Town.
All the eyes were shut.
Nid-dy and Nod-dy and White Dog
and Black Cat and Red Roos-ter and
Gray Squir-rel were all fast a-sleep.

Appendices

Appendix A:
After Reading Lessons Through Literature

After finishing all the levels of *Reading Lessons Through Literature*, you should be comfortable enough with the phonograms and the spelling rules to analyze any word you come across. Many people continue using this methodology to teach advanced spelling to their children. There are, however, different ways to do this.

If you wish to continue with advanced levels of *The Elson Readers*, you can dictate the new words from each story before your child reads it. *The Elson Readers* each have a word list at the end of the book listing all new words on each page.

The Ayres list is a list of the 1,000 most common words in the English language as determined by Leonard P. Ayres in the early 1900s. Because these words are so common, children who can spell them easily have an advantage in writing. The majority of the words were included in the previous spelling lists. The remaining 200+ words, unanalyzed and in alphabetical order, are on the following pages. These words, or other lists of common words, could be dictated to the child.

Prepared Dictation

We prefer a different method. We practice spelling through prepared dictation. Selections for prepared dictation are included in *Language Lessons Through Literature*, my grammar program. However, you can do prepared dictation with any text you like.

Dictation should not begin until third or fourth grade, depending on the readiness of the child. A child who has finished *Reading Lessons Through Literature* but who is not yet ready for dictation could analyze words from his copywork a few times a week instead.

In prepared dictation, children type or write a passage after studying it for five to ten minutes. The basic process was described by Charlotte Mason in her book *Home Education*. We combine the method with analyzing words according to phonograms and spelling rules.

I know that dictation can sound like a huge, time consuming exercise, especially with multiple children. It's not. We do prepared dictation twice a week, on the "off" days from grammar. First, I try to have my boys read through the spelling rules at least once each week, and we make an effort to analyze words that illustrate the different rules. (If they don't appear naturally through the passages we study, then we occasionally spend some time exploring a rule rather than a passage.) Then, each of my boys studies his passage for about ten minutes. He chooses, sometimes with my help, two or three words to analyze. A passage should not have more than three or four unknown words to be studied, though there's nothing wrong with analyzing extra words. He adds these to his Spelling Journal, analyzing each word syllable by syllable.

The Spelling Journal organizes words according to phonogram or spelling rule, and it is a free download on my site. The Spelling Journal can help identify problem spelling areas. Also, having children read through their Spelling Journals occasionally can help reinforce lessons from their previous studies. If you prefer to avoid printing out workbooks, then you could use the Spelling Journal as a template for creating a Spelling Journal in a composition book.

Dictations may be written or typed. My boys type their dictations. The spelling and grammar checks are turned off in our word processing program, and we increase the font size to 20+ points so that I can read over their shoulders. I read the exercises while each boy takes his turn at the keyboard. I stand behind them so that I can make sure they don't make any mistakes. When a mistake is made, we correct immediately. After the dictation, we analyze, or re-analyze, the missed word. Most weeks, there are no missed words from any of my boys.

Beginners can start with just a sentence or two, while older children can type or write up to several paragraphs. We use a variety of sources, including Aesop's fables, literature, Bible verses, poetry, and even my children's free reading choices. It's important to avoid passages which contain incorrect grammar, which many modern books do. However, I've found that dictation goes easier when the child is studying a passage he loves.

Appendix B:
The Remainder of the Ayres List

aboard

absence

accept

according

account

addition

address

adopt

affair

allege

although

annual

anyway

appear

application

appreciate

argument

arrangement

arrive

article

assist

associate

association

assure

athletic

attempt

attention

automobile

avenue

await

board

capture

career

celebration

character

circular

circumstance

citizen

clerk

collect

colonies

combination

command

committee

common

company

complaint

concern

condition

conference

connection

consider

consideration

contain

contract

convenient

convention

convict

cordially

death

debate

decision

degree

department

difference

different

difficulty

director

discussion

distinguish

distribute

district

divide

dollar

doubt

driven

drown

due

duty

earliest

education

effect | illustrate | official
effort | immediate | omit
elaborate | importance | opinion
emergency | important | organization
empire | impossible | organize
employ | imprison | particular
enclose | improvement | perfect
engage | include | period
engine | income | pleasure
entertain | increase | police
entitle | interest | political
entrance | investigate | popular
especially | invitation | preliminary
estate | issue | prepare
estimate | judgment | primary
evidence | justice | principal
experience | law | principle
extreme | madam | prison
factory | majority | proceed
feature | marriage | progress
figure | material | prompt
foreign | mayor | prove
forenoon | member | provide
form | mention | provision
forward | national | public
further | necessary | publication
general | objection | receipt
government | oblige | receive
himself | obtain | recent
history | occupy | recommend
husband | office | refer

Remainder of the Ayres List

reference	suppose
refuse	system
regard	terrible
region	testimony
relative	theater
relief	therefore
remain	thus
repair	unable
reply	understand
report	unfortunate
represent	vacation
respectfully	various
responsible	vessel
restrain	victim
retire	view
salary	whether
scene	
secretary	
section	
secure	
separate	
service	
session	
sincerely	
slower	
special	
statement	
steamer	
suffer	
summon	
supply	

Appendix C:
The Spelling Words in Alphabetical Order

This list of spelling words is in alphabetical order and shows in which lesson each word is analyzed. Lists 1-29 are in Level 1, lists 30-75 are in Level 2, and lists 76-127 are in Level 3.

Spelling Words in Alphabetical Order

Spelling Words in Alphabetical Order

Spelling Words in Alphabetical Order

Spelling Words in Alphabetical Order

Spelling Words in Alphabetical Order

Spelling Words in Alphabetical Order

Appendix D: Sample Schedules

The following pages have sample schedules. The charts show a detailed day to day plan for the first twelve weeks. The lists show an overview of the progression of all three levels.

Level 1: Spelling Lists 1-29

Level 2: Spelling Lists 30-75

Level 3: Spelling Lists 76-127

The first schedules are at the regular pace for starting with younger children, approximately Kindergarten age. This pace will take three years to complete three levels. The schedule begins teaching two phonograms per day and fifteen words per week.

The second schedules are at an accelerated pace for starting with older children, approximately first grade age. This pace will take two years to complete three levels. The schedule begins teaching four phonograms per day and twenty words per week.

Keep in mind, though, that you can and should adjust the pace to make the program work for you. The schedules are only here to give a general idea of how to use the program. Reduce the number of words down to only ten per week for a child who is overwhelmed by fifteen, or dictate only three words every day for a child who is overwhelmed by the writing. Increase the number of words for a child who needs more of a challenge.

The stories are not specifically scheduled. The child may read each story when he's covered the spelling list for the story and he's comfortable reading the words, even if he's still sounding them out. That will vary from child to child.

	Monday	Tuesday	Wednesday	Thursday	Friday
1	Learn c, a	Learn d, g Review Phonograms	Learn o, qu Phonogram Quiz	Learn i, j Review Phonograms	Learn m, n Phonogram Quiz
2	Learn r, l Review Phonograms	Learn h, k Review Phonograms	Learn b, p Phonogram Quiz	Learn t, u Review Phonograms	Learn y, e Phonogram Quiz
3	Learn f, s Review Phonograms	Learn v, w Review Phonograms	Learn x, z Phonogram Quiz	Learn th, ck Review Phonograms	Learn ai, ay Phonogram Quiz
4	Learn sh, ng Review Phonograms List 1-A (5 words)	Learn ee, oo Review Phonograms Read Spelling Words	Learn ou, ow Phonogram Quiz List 1-A (5 words), Read	Learn ar, ch Review Phonograms Read Spelling Words	Learn au, aw Phonogram Quiz List 1-B (5 words), Read
5	Learn oi, oy Review Phonograms List 1-B (5 words), Read	Learn er, ur Review Phonograms Read Spelling Words	Learn ir, ear Phonogram Quiz List 1-C (5 words), Read	Learn wor, wh Review Phonograms Read Spelling Words	Learn ea, or Phonogram Quiz List 1-C (5 words), Read
6	Learn ed, ew Review Phonograms List 1-D (5 words), Read	Learn cei, gu Review Phonograms Read Spelling Words	Learn wr, augh Phonogram Quiz List 1-D (5 words), Read	Learn ui, oa Review Phonograms Read Spelling Words	Learn ph, oe Phonogram Quiz List 1-E (5 words), Read

	Monday	Tuesday	Wednesday	Thursday	Friday
7	Learn tch, dge Review Phonograms List 1-E (5 words), Read	Learn ey, bu Review Phonograms Read Spelling Words	Learn ei, eigh Phonogram Quiz List 1-F (5 words), Read	Learn ci, ti Review Phonograms Read Spelling Words	Learn si, kn Phonogram Quiz List 1-F (5 words), Read
8	Learn igh, ie Review Phonograms List 1-G (5 words), Read	Learn gn, ough, mb Review Phonograms	Phonogram Quiz Read Spelling Words List 1-G (5 words)	Review Phonograms Read Spelling Words	Phonogram Quiz Read Spelling Words List 1-H (5 words)
9	Review Phonograms Read Spelling Words List 1-H (5 words)	Review Phonograms Read Spelling Words	Phonogram Quiz Read Spelling Words List 1-I (5 words)	Review Phonograms Read Spelling Words	Phonogram Quiz Read Spelling Words List 1-I (5 words)
10	Review Phonograms Read Spelling Words List 1-J (5 words)	Review Phonograms Read Spelling Words	Phonogram Quiz Read Spelling Words List 1-J (5 words)	Review Phonograms Read Spelling Words	Phonogram Quiz Read Spelling Words List 1-K (5 words)
11	Review Phonograms Read Spelling Words List 1-K (5 words)	Review Phonograms Read Spelling Words	Phonogram Quiz Read Spelling Words List 1-L (5 words)	Review Phonograms Read Spelling Words	Phonogram Quiz Read Spelling Words List 1-L (5 words)
12	Review Phonograms Read Spelling Words List 1-M (5 words)	Review Phonograms Read Spelling Words	Phonogram Quiz Read Spelling Words List 1-M (5 words)	Review Phonograms Read Spelling Words	Phonogram Quiz Read Spelling Words List 1-N (5 words)

Year 1

Week 1   Phonograms c through n

Week 2   Phonograms r through e

Week 3   Phonograms f through ay

Week 4   Phonograms sh through aw
          Spelling Lists: 1-A, half 1-B

Week 5   Phonograms oi through or
          Spelling Lists: half 1-B, 1-C

Week 6   Phonograms ed through oe
          Spelling Lists: 1-D, half 1-E

Week 7   Phonograms tch through kn
          Spelling Lists: half 1-E, 1-F

Week 8   Phonograms igh through mb
          Spelling Lists: 1-G, half 1-H

Week 9   Spelling Lists: half 1-H, 1-I

Week 10 Spelling Lists: 1-J, half 1-K

Week 11 Spelling Lists: half 1-K, 1-L

Week 12 Spelling Lists: 1-M, half 1-N

Week 13 Spelling Lists: half 1-N, 1-O

Week 14 Spelling Lists: 1-P, half 1-Q

Week 15 Spelling Lists: half 1-Q, 1-R

Week 16 Spelling Lists: 1-S, half 1-T

Week 17 Spelling Lists: half 1-T, 2

Week 18 Spelling Lists: 3, half 4

Week 19 Spelling Lists: half 4, 5

Week 20 Spelling Lists: 6, half 7

Week 21 Spelling Lists: half 7, 8

Week 22 Spelling Lists: 9, half 10

Week 23 Spelling Lists: half 10, 11

Week 24 Spelling Lists: 12, half 13

Week 25 Spelling Lists: half 13, 14

Week 26 Spelling Lists: 15, half 16

Week 27 Spelling Lists: half 16, 17

Week 28 Spelling Lists: 18, half 19

Week 29 Spelling Lists: half 19, 20

Week 30 Spelling Lists: 21, half 22

Week 31 Spelling Lists: half 22, 23

Week 32 Spelling Lists: 24, half 25

Week 33 Spelling Lists: half 25, 26

Week 34 Spelling Lists: 27, half 28

Week 35 Spelling Lists: half 28, 29

Year 2

Year 3

	Monday	Tuesday	Wednesday	Thursday	Friday
1	Learn c, a, d, g	Learn o, qu, i, j Review Phonograms	Learn m, n, r, l Phonogram Quiz	Learn h, k, b, p Review Phonograms	Learn t, u, y, e Phonogram Quiz
2	Learn f, s, v, w Review Phonograms	Learn x, z, th, ck Review Phonograms	Learn ai, ay, sh, ng Phonogram Quiz	Learn ee, oo, ou, ow Review Phonograms	Learn ar, ch, au, aw Phonogram Quiz
3	Learn oi, oy, er, ur Review Phonograms	Learn ir, ear, wor, wh Review Phonograms	Learn ea, or, ed, ew Phonogram Quiz	Learn cei, gu, wr, augh Review Phonograms	Learn ui, oa, ph, oe Phonogram Quiz
4	Learn tch, dge, ey, bu Review Phonograms	Learn ei, eigh, ci, ti Review Phonograms List 1-A	Learn si, kn, igh, ie Phonogram Quiz Read Spelling Words	Learn gn, ough, mb Review Phonograms List 1-B	Phonogram Quiz Read Spelling Words
5	Review Phonograms Read Spelling Words	Review Phonograms List 1-C	Phonogram Quiz Read Spelling Words	Review Phonograms List 1-D	Phonogram Quiz Read Spelling Words
6	Review Phonograms Read Spelling Words	Review Phonograms List 1-E	Phonogram Quiz Read Spelling Words	Review Phonograms List 1-F	Phonogram Quiz Read Spelling Words

	Monday	Tuesday	Wednesday	Thursday	Friday
7	Review Phonograms Read Spelling Words	Review Phonograms List 1-G	Phonogram Quiz Read Spelling Words Phonogram Quiz	Review Phonograms List 1-H Review Phonograms	Phonogram Quiz Read Spelling Words Phonogram Quiz
8	Review Phonograms Read Spelling Words	Review Phonograms List 1-I	Read Spelling Words	Read Spelling Words List 1-J	Read Spelling Words
9	Review Phonograms Read Spelling Words	Review Phonograms Read Spelling Words List 1-K	Phonogram Quiz Read Spelling Words	Review Phonograms Read Spelling Words List 1-L	Phonogram Quiz Read Spelling Words
10	Review Phonograms Read Spelling Words	Review Phonograms Read Spelling Words List 1-M	Phonogram Quiz Read Spelling Words	Review Phonograms Read Spelling Words List 1-N	Phonogram Quiz Read Spelling Words
11	Review Phonograms Read Spelling Words	Review Phonograms Read Spelling Words List 1-O	Phonogram Quiz Read Spelling Words	Review Phonograms Read Spelling Words List 1-P	Phonogram Quiz Read Spelling Words
12	Review Phonograms Read Spelling Words	Review Phonograms Read Spelling Words List 1-Q	Phonogram Quiz Read Spelling Words	Review Phonograms Read Spelling Words List 1-R	Phonogram Quiz Read Spelling Words

Year 1

Week 1   Phonograms c through e

Week 2   Phonograms f through aw

Week 3   Phonograms oi through oe

Week 4   Phonograms tch through mb

            Spelling Lists: 1-A, 1-B

Week 5   Capitals c through e

            Spelling Lists: 1-C, 1-D

Week 6   Capitals f through z

            Spelling Lists: 1-E, 1-F

Week 7   Spelling Lists: 1-G, 1-H

Week 8   Spelling Lists: 1-I, 1-J

Week 9   Spelling Lists: 1-K, 1-L

Week 10 Spelling Lists: 1-M, 1-N

Week 11 Spelling Lists: 1-O, 1-P

Week 12 Spelling Lists: 1-Q, 1-R

Week 13 Spelling Lists: 1-S, 1-T

Week 14 Spelling Lists: 2-3

Week 15 Spelling Lists: 4-5

Week 16 Spelling Lists: 6-7

Week 17 Spelling Lists: 8-9

Week 18 Spelling Lists: 10-11

Week 19 Spelling Lists: 12-13

Week 20 Spelling Lists: 14-15

Week 21 Spelling Lists: 16-17

Week 22 Spelling Lists: 18-19

Week 23 Spelling Lists: 20-21

Week 24 Spelling Lists: 22-23

Week 25 Spelling Lists: 24-25

Week 26 Spelling Lists: 26-27

Week 27 Spelling Lists: 28-29

Week 28 Spelling Lists: 30-31

Week 29 Spelling Lists: 32-33

Week 30 Spelling Lists: 34-35

Week 31 Spelling Lists: 36-37

Week 32 Spelling Lists: 38-39

Week 33 Spelling Lists: 40-41

Week 34 Spelling Lists: 42-43

Week 35 Spelling Lists: 44-45

Week 36 Spelling Lists: 46-47

Year 2

Appendix E: Advanced Phonograms

Some of the basic phonograms have advanced sounds. In those cases, all of the sounds of the phonogram are mentioned in this list. Also, many words with advanced phonograms could also be explained with silent letters or as exceptions.

ae	/ā/, /ē/, /ĕ/	aerial, algae, aesthetic
ah	/ä/	blah
ai	/ā/, /ī/, /ă/	mail, aisle, plaid
au	/ä/, /ō/, /ā/, /ow/	aunt, chauffeur, gauge, sauerkraut
ay	/ā/, /ī/	day, cayenne
cc	/ch/	cappuccino
ce	/sh/	ocean
cu	/k/, /kw/	biscuit, cuisine
eau	/ō/, /ū/, /ŏ/	bureau, beauty, bureaucracy
ei	/ā/, /ē/, /ī/, /ĭ/, /ĕ/	their, protein, feisty, forfeit, heifer
et	/ā/	ballet
eu	/oo/, /ū/	neutral, feud
ey	/ā/, /ē/, /ī/	they, turkey, geyser
ge	/j/, /zh/	surgeon, mirage
gh	/g/	ghost
gn	/n/	gnome
oe	/ō/, /oo/, /ē/	toe, shoe, subpoena
ot	/ō/	depot
our	/er/	journey
pn	/n/	pneumonia
ps	/s/	psalm
pt	/t/	pterodactyl
qu	/kw/, /k/	critique
rh	/r/	rhyme
sc	/s/	science
sci	/ch/	conscience
th	/th/, /TH/, /t/	thought, them, thyme
ut	/ū/	debut
x	/ks/, /z/	box, xylophone
yr	/ēr/, /er/	lyric, syrup
z	/z/, /s/	zoo, quartz